RETURNING TO WRIGHT STREET

RETURNING TO WRIGHT STREET

COVER PHOTO: 1200 block of Wright Street looking north toward Morris Street (circa 1950). Author's house at 1218 Wright has low hedges around front yard just to left of center photo.

ISBN # 978-0-9845794-5-7

Printed in the United States of America

First edition: 2010

Typeface: Book Antigua

The Publishing Place
www.thePubPlace.com

RETURNING TO WRIGHT STREET

More Life, Love, and Laughs of a City Boy Growing Up in the 1940s and '50s

Charles Edward White

Charles Edward White

A Note to the Reader

Hello—or hello again. This is my second book about growing up while living at 1218 Wright Street in the Fountain Square area on the south side of Indianapolis during the 1940s and '50s. I decided to write it because more and more memories kept coming to mind after my first book, *Remembering Wright Street,* was published in August 2009.

Many of you were generous in your praise of *Remembering* and encouraged me to share more of my true stories and personal essays. Your encouragement led to the writing of the book you're holding in your hands.

I hope you'll enjoy *Returning to Wright Street*. It's written in the same easy-to-read style as my first book. If this is your initial exposure to my memories of that special time and place I grew up in, I hope that after reading *Returning* you'll want to go back and read *Remembering*. It's another journey worth taking.

—C.E.W.

CONTACT INFO:

Mailing address:
3052 Trailwood Lane, Lexington, KY 40511

E-mail: chuckwhite57@insightbb.com

Phone: (859) 231-0007

NOTE: *Remembering Wright Street* is still available for $14.95 (plus $3 postage). Make your check out to Charles Edward White and mail to the above address.

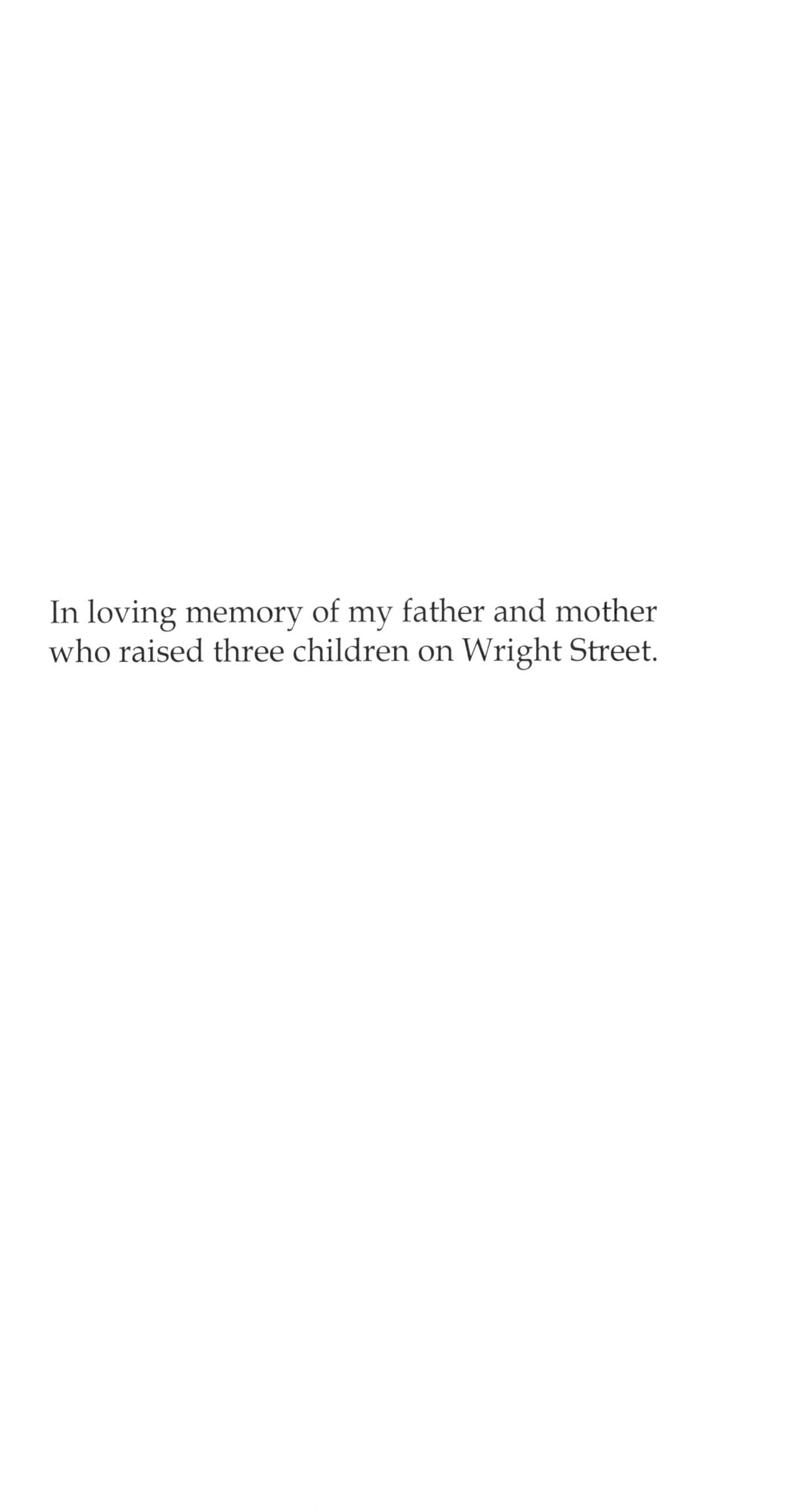

In loving memory of my father and mother
who raised three children on Wright Street.

Jackie (3), Sandy (4-1/2), and me (7). This is the only childhood photo taken of us together by a professional photographer.

Acknowledgments

I appreciate the help Dale Mortenbeck (Manual Class of '56) provided both as a researcher and contributor of additional material to this and my previous book. He started out as just a kid I didn't even know while growing up in my old neighborhood, but during the writing of these two books he has become a real friend. Thanks, Dale.

Much appreciation also goes to my publisher, Jenny Holmes Pemberton, for her tireless effort and patience in working with me to prepare this and my previous book for publication. Her professional expertise and personal friendship are two things I've come to truly treasure. Thanks, Jen.

I also greatly appreciate the help given to me by my faithful crew of encouragers and manuscript reviewers: Shelley Adams, Sandy (White) Foster, Ken Fuller, Don Hughes, Su Shortridge, Mary Wade, and Jackie (White) Whitney. As a result of their combined work, this book turned out even better than I hoped it would. Thanks, gang.

Last of all, let me express my appreciation to those of you who read my first book and urged me to write another one sharing more about my growing-up years on Wright Street. Your compliments and encouragement meant a lot to me and resulted in the writing of this second book of memories. My thanks to each of you.

Contents

Introduction

Raised on Wright Street

When we're born, we have absolutely no control over who our parents will be, where we'll live, or how we'll be raised as children. As it turned out, I was extremely fortunate in all three of these categories. I had parents who loved me. We lived in a succession of homes on the near south side of Indianapolis, Indiana. And my folks did their best to raise me and my two sisters right. Most of those growing-up years were spent living on Wright Street. Here's how it came about.

There was a young man named Clifford Howard White from Stilesville, an insignificant little country crossroads town on U. S. 40 in Hendricks County, west of Indianapolis. While in his twenties, Cliff (as most everyone called him) moved to the big city of Indianapolis to seek his fortune. One day he was back in his home town visiting a good friend. While there, his friend's wife introduced Cliff to her younger sister. Her name was Evelyn Veda Ayres and she lived on the south side of Indianapolis. Cliff was 27; Evelyn was only 19. But they quickly fell in love and in less than a year they were married on April 30, 1938. A few days short of nine months later, I was born. And, yes, that truly made me a "honeymoon baby."

At the time of my birth, my parents were renting a small apartment in a house on the northeast corner of Wright and Sanders streets. This was in a typical working-class neighborhood west of Fountain Square. During my first year of life, my folks moved over to the upper level of a duplex in the seven-hundred block of Morris Street. A year or so after I came along, my sister, Sandra Lee, was born and our parents decided they needed more room for their growing family. So, we moved several blocks further west to a rental house at 1710 Union Street. After we'd settled in there for another year or so, our folks added a baby sister to our family. Her name was Jacqueline Sue. Now, there were five of us.

I lived on Union Street until sometime during the summer of 1945. Few memories of those early days have stayed with me. One of my earliest recollections is walking a block up the street to a kindergarten operated by the nuns at Sacred Heart Catholic Church. In those days, many kindergartens were privately operated—mostly by churches—and weren't part of the school system. At the time, I didn't think anything of it, but when I grew older I came to realize something: our family was *not* Catholic. I guess because this was the closest available kindergarten, my parents decided on convenience over conviction.

I have only two clear memories of my kindergarten days. One memory is of women in strange black-shrouded outfits and chunky black shoes moving among their flock of little children. My other memory is making red-and-green construction paper chains—I can still smell that white paste—and hanging them around our classroom as Christmas decorations. Even though I was the only Protestant boy in Sacred Heart's kindergarten, I survived my preschool experience there with no ill effects. But I still wonder what my parents thought when I crossed myself one night after Dad said grace before supper.

The next stage in my scholastic adventure was starting to elementary school the following year at P. S. #22. This was a fairly new school just a couple of blocks north and three blocks west of where I lived. I have only two memories of attending first grade there. The first is walking up the east side of busy South Meridian Street and shouting back and forth as traffic whizzed by in both directions. The object of my attempted conversations was a boy in my grade named Danny Chapell. He lived somewhere west of Meridian, but I wasn't allowed to cross over until I came to the marked crosswalk in the school zone. From there we walked together the last block to the school building. Danny was probably my first friend. I liked being around him because he was a happy kid.

My other memory of P. S. #22 is not such a pleasant one. There was a certain mean boy (I don't recall his name) who used to threaten to beat me up unless I gave him my lunch money. Evidently, I believed his threats and surrendered my coins on a regular basis. He must have had several of us paying him off, since he graciously only collected from each of us one day a week. At least I got to eat lunch *most* of the time. I kept quiet about this situation until questioned by my mother why I came home so hungry on a certain day of the week. I broke down and told her about the boy taking my lunch money. Mom was really upset that such a thing could happen to me at school. She must have gone to the principal and complained about the matter because shortly after that the boy quit bothering me. He never did beat me up, but he sure gave me some dirty looks. I don't know if the lunch money extortionist was a cause or not, but we moved at the end of my first semester.

This time my parents relocated back to the same street they'd lived on when they were first married. They rented a three-bedroom house for nine months and then convinced the owner to sell it to them for $6,500 (payments were $45 per month). This place was located within half a block of their honeymoon home. Our new address was 1218 Wright Street. I lived there from the age of six-and-a-half until I was twenty, married my high school sweetheart, and moved out on my own. And that's how I came to live on Wright Street for the fourteen-year period covering my childhood, teen years, and first year as a young man.

The southern four blocks of Wright Street (from Sanders down to Cottage) still remain, but the northern four blocks (from Buchanan down to Sanders) was erased from the map back in the mid-1960s. In the name of progress, this and the surrounding area containing hundreds of homes was replaced with a huge interchange between Interstates 65 and 70. Unfortunately, my house in the block between Morris and Sanders was included in the zone of destruction. As a result, I can no longer return to the street I grew up on, walk along its shaded sidewalks, or revisit the house I was raised in. Those long-missing blocks of Wright Street now exist only in the hearts and minds of those who once lived along them, or on one of the several other streets in the Fountain Square neighborhood that were also wiped out back in the '60s.

The following random memories are drawn from my years of living on that street during the 1940s and '50s. The true stories and personal essays in this book appear in chronological order. They fill in many of the gaps between the chapters in my first book, *Remembering Wright Street*. The pages you are about to read tell about more memorable people, unusual events, and special places and things I remember from back then. So, with all that said, let's begin our journey back through the years and across the miles. We're now returning to Wright Street as it was . . . and will never be again.

School #22 was located on the east side of Illinois Street (a block west of South Meridian Street in the second block south of West Morris Street) between Kansas and Wisconsin streets. No trace of the school building remains today and grass is growing where it once stood. Other structures have been built over the years on the empty block once occupied by the school and its playground.

1200 block of Wright Street looking north
(circa 1950).

My family's house at 1218 Wright Street
(circa 1950).

Me and my sisters Jackie (left) and Sandy (right) with Dad in the middle out in our front yard. Mom was taking the photo.

Me and Sandy and Jackie at a state park somewhere in Indiana when we were teenagers. And, no, our legs were not abnormally long. The photo must have been distorted because it was taken looking uphill. Note the Roy Rogers binoculars hanging around our necks.

1

Getting Clipped

During the first few years of my life, my hair was blond and curly—really blond, really curly. So much so that, today, when looking at childhood photos of myself taken back then, I can hardly believe it's really me. My paternal grandfather, who died before I was born, had been a professional barber most of his life. Dad must have inherited some of his father's hair-cutting skill and used it to trim my hair now and then at home. My hair finally grew to a length where he could no longer keep it trimmed to suit my mother. Besides, the blond color was darkening to a light brown and the curls looked too babyish for a boy my age. This resulted in my reaching that time in life that every boy's mother dreads: when her son gets his first real haircut at a barbershop and loses his baby curls forever.

I'm not sure how old I was when this time came for me, maybe around four. But I remember the incident quite well—and for a very valid reason. One wintry day, Dad took me to a barbershop down on the south side of Raymond

Street a couple doors east of South Meridian. Since I was just a little kid, the barber placed a special board across the arms of his barber chair to boost me higher. After I climbed up on the board seat, the barber wrapped a strip of white tissue paper around my neck. Then, he covered me up with a big, white sheet to keep the hair off my clothes.

So far, so good. But I was half afraid, as any child might be, of undergoing something I'd never previously experienced. After all, Dad had always cut my hair before, so why should I trust this guy—a total stranger—to do it? As long as I was facing my father, I was okay. But when the barber turned me slightly and I couldn't see Dad I got antsy.

I kept trying to twist my head around to see Dad. The barber, gently at first and then with increasing force, kept turning my head back around. He said several times, "Hold still, now. Don't move your head."

Large windows, partly steamed up with condensation, covered much of the shop's front wall. Raymond Street was a major thoroughfare with lots of traffic zipping by. Suddenly, a fire engine came roaring down the street with its siren wailing and bell clanging. Naturally, this caught my attention and I whipped my head around to see it. Unfortunately, I did this while the barber was trimming over my right ear.

OOOWWW! He caught the edge of my

ear in his sharp scissors and nipped me good. My hand shot up to the site of my injury and pain. When I took my hand down, I saw blood on my fingers. That was enough for me. Before the barber or Dad could stop me, I jumped down out of the barber chair, dashed across the shop, out the door, and started running down the sidewalk as fast as I could with the cloth cover flapping around me. It's a wonder I didn't trip over it. I almost made it clear to Meridian before my dad caught me. Good thing he did. I don't know what I would've done had I made it to the corner. In my childish panic, I might've kept running right out into traffic. And that could've resulted in my trip to the barbershop being both my first and my last.

Dad held my wrist firmly and began trying to tow me back to the scene of the crime. He wasn't making much progress because I was crying and protesting loudly all the way; I was pitching a real fit. Then, Dad noticed I was bleeding. He stopped, knelt down, and pulled out his pocket hanky. As he put it up to my ear, he said, "I know it hurts, son. But it'll be alright. Trust me." And with those words he gave me a reassuring hug. Then, he picked me up in his arms and carried me the rest of the way back down the street to the shop.

I quieted down by the time we went inside, but I was still sniffling. The barber told my father he was really sorry and reminded him that I'd been told repeatedly to hold still and not move my head. Now I knew why. He said it wouldn't take him much longer to finish my haircut as Dad sat me back on the board atop the barber chair. The barber told me that if I'd be good and not move any more he'd give me a sucker when he was done. That sounded worth shutting up and sitting still for. So, I did.

I was still holding Dad's hanky against my ear. Before resuming my haircut, the barber said, "Let's see how bad the damages are." He carefully pulled the hanky away and looked at my wounded ear. "Hmmm. I think we can fix that," he said. "Now, this might sting a little," he said as he put some white powdered stuff on my ear (I figured out years later it was alum) to stop the bleeding.

The barber was right; it *did* sting. In fact, it stung enough that I almost started crying again, but only for a few seconds. Dad stood next to me while I was in the chair and I held back my tears because I could see my father's smiling face and knew everything was going to be okay like he'd said. And, besides, I wanted that sucker I was promised.

I sat there and didn't move a muscle; I hardly blinked my eyes. Five minutes or so later, the barber finished my first professional haircut with no further problems. The last thing he did was squirt some good-smelling, green juice out of a tall bottle and work it into my hair with his fingers. I liked that part of my haircut best of all. A few quick motions with the comb and he was done. Bet he was sure glad that was over. I know I was.

Before the barber removed the sheet, Dad picked up a curl of my hair and stuck it in a small envelope he'd brought with him. He said, "Your mother asked me to bring her this to put in your album." At the time I didn't know why she'd want it, but years later I found out it was a traditional thing that many mothers did.

As I watched in the mirror, I saw the barber smile as he pulled away the sheet and snapped it a couple of times to remove my hair clippings. After unwinding the tissue paper strip, he shook some powder into a brush and whisked it all around my neck and ears while protecting my wounded ear with his left hand. After I climbed down out of the chair, the barber kept his word and rewarded me with my pick of suckers from a big glass jar. I grabbed a red one. The cherry-flavored sucker tasted good, but I felt like I'd earned it. Maybe I should've asked him for *two* suckers.

When we got back home, I quickly told my mother how the mean old barber man had cut my ear and showed her my wound. Mom, of course, was very sympathetic and kissed me on the forehead. She taped some gauze over my ear so I wouldn't pick at it or rub it on my pillow at night. The nick healed up in a few days with no problems or aftereffects. Well, there was one. I ended up with a tiny notch in the top edge of my right ear. Sixty-five years later, the notch is barely visible, but it's still there. Whenever I absent-mindedly rub the edge of my ear, I can feel that notch today and remember how I received it when a young boy. And you know what? I *still* think I deserved a second sucker.

The long white, frame building along the south side of Raymond Street that housed the barbershop and a couple of other businesses was torn down many years ago when Raymond was widened to accommodate more lanes of traffic.

Me and my golden locks at about age 2 (a couple years before losing them to that mean old barber).

2

Memories of a World at War

The majority of people alive today think of World War II as just another event from the history books. An occasional new war movie reminds the public that once upon a time there was a long and terrible conflict fought by two groups of nations—the evil Axis powers and the Allies—on many battlefields around the world. Those from my generation, however, remember WWII as something we actually lived through and experienced. The war wasn't history to us at the time; it was current events on a day-by-day basis for nearly four years of our young lives.

When I was born on January 25, 1939, WWII hadn't yet begun, although events were already taking place that would soon lead to it in September of that year. By the time the war finally ended on August 15, 1945, I was just a little over six-and-a-half-years-old. During those few years of my life as a young boy, I lived through the greatest war the world has ever known. At such an impressionable age, I stored away many memories of WWII on the home front. You won't find many of these in the history books.

Rationing of foods such as meat, butter, chocolate, sugar, cooking oil and fats, cheese, dried beans, coffee, canned goods—even ketchup—was controlled by a government agency called the OPA (Office of Price Administration). Besides food, other scarce items were also rationed. These included soap, gasoline, tires, and shoes. The government issued rationing stamp books and purchases of rationed items could only be made with the appropriate number of stamps—*if* the item was even available for purchase. I may not have understood exactly what rationing meant, but I can remember Mom tearing out those little stamps (about half the size of a regular postage stamp) at the grocery store in order to buy certain items. Each food or other category had a different color stamp: red, orange, yellow, blue, green, black, or brown. Small tokens (some red, some blue, and about the size of dimes) made of pressed paper were used by the grocer to return "change" if the item purchased cost less than the value of the stamp. Mom kept her stamp books hidden in a corner of the kitchen cupboard—they were more valuable than money. Rationing was a way of life for the duration of the war. It was implemented to prevent overbuying, hoarding, and to discourage black-market profiteering. My family always had enough to eat during the war; I don't remember ever going hungry.

Saving scrap materials for use in the war became the duty of every American citizen. After emptying the contents out of a tin can, Mom would rinse it out thoroughly and then open the bottom of the can. She would fold both ends inside the can and I had the duty of stepping on the can to flatten it. We saved the cans in a cardboard box in the bottom of the china cabinet in the kitchen. When the box was full, Dad would take it somewhere and turn in the cans for use in the war effort. Besides our tin cans, we also collected other scrap metal and saved our old newspapers. We were proud to do our part in patriotic recycling for the good of the cause.

Learning to eat something called oleomargarine in place of butter is another fond war memory. This stuff came sealed in a plastic bag with a round, red capsule in the center. You would break the capsule by squeezing it, then knead the bag until the coloring worked its way through the white contents and turned it a buttery yellow. My sisters and I would take turns squeezing the bag and thought it was fun to see the color change like magic. Real butter wasn't available again until after the war.

A not-so-happy memory was seeing the Western Union messenger boy riding his bicycle down the street and wondering what family he might be taking bad news to regarding a loved one serving in the armed forces. So many men and women died, were wounded, captured, or missing in action during the war that the various services couldn't spare the manpower to deliver such notifications. Western Union must have been very, very busy during those years.

I remember seeing a red and blue "E for Excellence" flag flying from the pole over the main entrance of the Pittman-Moore Pharmaceutical Company at the corner of Morris Street and Madison Avenue. These banners were awarded by the federal government to companies meeting or exceeding their war production goals.

New cars became a thing of the past for the duration of the war as car builders converted their production lines to building jeeps, tanks, and airplanes. My father kept our old Studebaker Champion and drove it throughout the war. When the original light blue paint became dull and faded, he had it repainted a shiny black. It looked like a new car, but was the same old one under the paint job.

Blue star and gold star banners hung proudly in the front windows of many homes in our neighborhood. Each blue star represented a family member serving in the armed forces. A gold star symbolized one who had given his or her life in the service of America and her allies. Some of these banners had two or even three stars on them. These families made the ultimate sacrifice.

Air raid drills were held regularly and always at night. This made them extra exciting. Loud sirens would wail across the city and every house would turn their lights off or down, and cover all windows. Air raid wardens ran up and down the streets checking their neighbor's houses. This was the only time during the war when I can remember being frightened. It was scary sitting inside your house in the dark or with the lights turned down low and the curtains drawn so as not to give away the location of our city to enemy bombers. Of course, the great distances across the oceans protected America, especially its heartland where we lived. But we still feared the remote possibility of being bombed by the evil Nazis.

Trainloads of tanks, half-tracks, and artillery pieces on railroad flatcars were seen frequently. Other trains carried servicemen on their way to various training camps around the country—or to a port city where they would sail away to some distant war zone. These were always exciting things for a young boy to see at railroad crossings.

American flags were flown from most front porches every day. Flag sales must have soared during the war years. It seemed like everyone had a flag and showed their patriotism by flying it regularly.

Commercial advertising incorporated war

themes. Coca-Cola issued a series of posters showing various U. S. military airplanes, some in combat situations. My dad knew someone who worked in Coke's advertising department. His friend gave me two sets of ten posters each. I hung them on the walls of my bedroom. All my buddies thought the posters were really neat. My lifelong interest in WWII aircraft no doubt grew from this beginning.

Newsreels at the movies always included the latest war news. There were also reminders to be patriotic and "Buy War Bonds" to finance the great cost of the war. War films often replaced the usual westerns and cops-and-robbers stories. The war movies were my favorites and made me hope the war lasted long enough for me to grow up and go fight the bad guys. How naïve a six year-old can be.

Basic housing was hurriedly constructed in the Mars Hill area on the southwest side of town to provide homes for the thousands of people working at the nearby Allison's plant and other defense industries. This housing area was sometimes referred to as Dog Town. Don't ask me why. Maybe because there were no fenced yards and peoples' dogs ran loose.

Occasionally, I'd see military airplanes flying over the city. Some were based out at Stout Field on Holt Road. I especially remember the P-51 Mustangs which were my favorite U. S. airplane during the war.

My family's personal connection with the war was Dad's brother, my Uncle James, who was in the Army Air Force (as it was called in those days). When he came to visit us on leave, he brought me official military cloth patches of the various air force commands. I ended up with a complete set that made me the envy of other boys.

After the war, a good friend of my father gave me a genuine Nazi swastika armband he said he'd taken off a dead German soldier. The edge of it was torn. He told me that was where his bayonet had sliced into it (he may have been pulling my leg about that). In any case, I was greatly impressed by this authentic souvenir from the war.

This was World War II through the eyes of a young boy. The words "all gave some and some gave all" come to mind whenever I think back to those early years of my life. These words apply not only to the servicemen and women who fought in the war, but to those of us who remained behind on the home front. Every American made sacrifices to a greater or lesser degree. Tens of thousands serving in the military made the greatest sacrifice of all: their lives. Their families on the home front lost husbands, sons, and brothers. Hundreds of thousands of the veterans who survived the war came home missing limbs and with other physical wounds, as well as emotional conditions from which they would never recover. It was a terrible price to pay in order to rid the world of tyranny and persecution. But the price was paid and the victory was won.

I guess I should consider myself fortunate for never being called to serve in the armed forces after I grew up during the days of the draft. As I've grown older, I've often wished that I *had* been called—especially when the stirring anthems of the various branches of military service are played at special ceremonies honoring our veterans. When I see the shrinking numbers of those older men and women who fought in World War II standing with pride—and sometimes tears—in their eyes, I wish that I could stand with them. But I and other civilians deserve no such honor. Our sacrifices were nothing compared to theirs, and to the others who never came home from the war.

Yes, I was only a little kid who lived out the war on the home front. But that experience caused me to grow up having the greatest respect and admiration for all military veterans of World War II, as well as from all the other armed conflicts in which America has been involved since then. God bless them all.

3

When the Church Bells Rang All Day

Every adult American alive today has heard of World War II and knows that the U. S. was on the winning side. Many of them, however, may not know or remember that this greatest of all wars actually had a *double* ending. The first occurred when Nazi Germany was defeated by the Allies in Europe; the second came a few months later when imperialist Japan finally surrendered in the Pacific. Today, over sixty years later, I can still remember both these history-making endings of World War II.

During most of the war, my family lived at 1710 Union Street (two blocks east of South Meridian and a few blocks south of East Morris). Even though I wasn't quite six-and-a-half-years-old and didn't know the date at the time (it was May 8, 1945), I remember what was called V-E (Victory in Europe) Day. The streets and sidewalks were still wet from a spring shower that had just ended after drenching the south side of Indianapolis. We heard the church bells start ringing up the street at Sacred Heart

Catholic Church. Others began ringing off in the distance. Then we noticed car horns were honking over on Meridian Street. The few that drove down Union Street honked theirs as well. Something unusual had obviously happened. Mom excitedly turned on the radio just as the newscaster was repeating the announcement that all America had been waiting to hear: the Allies had defeated Nazi Germany. Hooray! The war in Europe was over.

Most of our neighbors of all ages came out on their porches or into their yards; everyone began celebrating. Many were banging on pots and pans with wooden spoons while others clanged the lids together to celebrate the wonderful news. One neighbor lady had an old cowbell she kept shaking. A few of the older boys on our street set off some firecrackers they'd stashed away for the occasion (explosive fireworks were still legal back in those days). We younger children ran up and down the sidewalks along our street yelling and making all the noise we could. Some kids were waving little American flags.

We kids knew the war that had been going on during most or all of our young lives had ended in a place called Europe. But at our age we didn't really know where Europe was or understand fully what the war was all about. We just knew it was far across the ocean somewhere and that a bad man named Hitler had started it. But, in any case, we enjoyed all the excitement. In my enthusiasm I jumped into some puddles on the sidewalk and splashed water on my two sisters. They didn't like it, and Mom told me to stop. Then, suddenly, I had something in my eye. Whatever it was really hurt and I began crying. But my tears wouldn't wash it out.

Dad was at work, so Mom tried to look in my eye. I was crying so hard she couldn't force my eyelid open. A man we knew who lived a couple doors up the street heard me carrying on and asked my mother what was wrong. She told him and he said to bring me over to his porch. Mom quickly led me to his house while I continued sobbing. The man said he knew an old trick that would help solve my problem. He went inside and came back out with a wooden kitchen match. He motioned me over to him. I was curious, but afraid and wondered, *What's he going to do with that match, stick it in my eye and burn out whatever is hurting me?* Unrealistic childhood fear can imagine anything.

The man quieted me down with some reassuring words. Then, he held the match sideways and used it to roll back my upper eyelid. Now he could see what was in my eye and dabbed at it with the corner of his hanky. The object was a small flake of soot that must have blown out of a chimney. After blinking a few times, the pain was gone. Boy, my eye sure felt better. I thanked the helpful neighbor man and immediately ran to rejoin the other kids in the ongoing celebration. And that's my entire recollection of V-E Day. Here the whole world was celebrating the defeat of Germany and all I could think about for a few agonizing minutes was having something in my eye.

Sometime during the next couple of months (most likely after school was out in June), my family moved from our rented house on Union Street to another one over on Wright Street. One afternoon in the dog days of summer, I remember hearing another announcement about the war on our radio. Again, I didn't know the date (it was August 15th). This time the newscaster said that after America had dropped a second "atomic bomb" on Japan, they had finally surrendered. At last! The war in the Pacific was over. I had no idea what an atomic bomb was, but I remember thinking that it must have been a really, really big and powerful one to end the war after we dropped only *two* of them on the Japs. I overheard some adults talking about the bombs and saying that those dirty Japs got what they deserved for their sneak attack on Pearl Harbor, whatever that meant.

On what was known as V-J (Victory over Japan) Day, the church bells near and far again began ringing joyously and kept it up for hours. The bells at St. John's E. & R. Church on Sanders Street were the closest and loudest. But we could also hear St. Pat's bells from over toward Fountain Square and others off in the distance. People were tooting their car horns and neighbors came out of their houses to celebrate the victory. I don't remember as much clanging of pots and pans or setting off of firecrackers this time.

The V-J Day celebration wasn't nearly as boisterous and didn't last as long as the one following our victory over Germany—at least not in our neighborhood. Maybe people were just relieved that the whole thing was finally over after nearly four years of fighting. Or, maybe it was just too darn hot to get as worked up over as people had back in May when the Nazis surrendered. This time I didn't get anything in my eye to interfere with my enjoyment of participating in the celebration of the second and final ending of World War II.

The stars and stripes flown at nearly every house rippled proudly in the hot summer breeze blowing along Wright Street that day as we celebrated America's greatest victory.

There was one other occasion during my childhood when the church bells rang all day. The date was April 12, 1945, the day President Franklin D. Roosevelt died. The bells were rung in a more somber manner that day than they were on V-E and V-J Day. Their slow, deep tones expressed the great sadness of America for its fallen leader, a sadness shared by our Allies around the world.

4

A Boy's Toys

Toys have always amused and fascinated children. That's why kids love them. Certain types of toys also help to develop children's imagination and creativity. While growing up on Wright Street, I had my share of just plain fun toys, but enjoyed the educational kind most of all. Several of these were construction sets that involved building things out of standardized component parts.

The earliest of these was a set of Tinker-Toys. These sets came in a large variety of sizes; mine was a middle-size set packaged in a heavy cardboard cylinder with a screw-on metal cap. Tinker-Toys were an assortment of nicely finished wooden rods about the diameter of a pencil and in various lengths from one-inch up to twelve-inches in two-inch increments. The rods were made to fit into various types of connectors, also made of wood. My set included a few other special accessory pieces and an idea booklet showing several things that could be built with its pieces. After completing all those, I had even more fun creating my own unique structures.

Next came another construction set called Buildo. After World War II ended and aluminum was no longer needed for manufacturing warplanes it became available for making toys. The Buildo set consisted of aluminum pieces of assorted sizes and shapes. These could be bolted together to create a variety of different machines and structures. The set came with a large supply of tiny nuts and bolts for this purpose, along with a screwdriver and a wrench. A booklet was included showing projects to build, but I often used my imagination to come up with things not in the book. Believe it or not, after all these years, I still have a few pieces from this set (see photo).

After the Buildo set, I moved up to what most boys really wanted: an Erector set. This was the absolute ultimate in building sets. The Erector set included an assortment of stamped-out steel pieces resembling girders and other structural elements. Different size sets were available with increasing numbers of pieces and accessories. My set was a midline model which included an electric motor, several gears, axles, pulleys, and wheels to make power-driven machines. Like Buildo, Erector sets also used tiny nuts and bolts to assemble the pieces into quite elaborate structures. The more expensive sets came in nice metal carrying cases; my set came in a cardboard box. But I still had hours of fun building things with it. Today, in a box of miscellaneous metal junk that I keep out in my garage, I still have a few odds and ends (see photo) from my old Erector set that I played with as a boy sixty-some years ago. How's that for durability?

Another construction-type toy I enjoyed as a boy was a set of American Logs. These were pre-notched, brown-stained miniature "logs" in various lengths which could be used to construct cabins, forts, and other such structures. The logs in my set had a square cross-section; another, more popular, brand called Lincoln Logs had circular logs. Interlocking green roof boards were included in my set, along with red wooden chimneys. The possibilities were more limited with the toy logs than with the other construction-type sets, but I still managed to create some unusual structures with them. Since they were made of solid wood they were another truly indestructible toy that never wore out.

Back in those days long before LEGO was ever heard of, the closest thing to it that I had to play with was another construction set called American Bricks. These were molded of plastic, but weren't smooth like LEGO. Instead, they had a textured surface to make them seem more like real bricks. Most were red with some accessory pieces in white (to look more like concrete for foundations, window and door headers, etc.). The plastic pieces snapped together similarly to LEGO. A couple of green cardboard roofs with embossed patterns of shingles were included, along with plastic doors and windows that really opened and closed. I quickly became bored with building nothing but houses, so began improvising all sorts of other structures. I was limited in what I could create by the small variety of shapes in the set. If LEGO had been available in my day, there would have been no limits to my creativity with it. Of course, I didn't even know that such a thing as LEGO would ever exist, so I was content as a boy to build what I could with my set of plastic bricks.

In addition to these various construction sets, I also had an electric train. Like every boy, I dreamt of getting a Lionel train. Lionel built the most realistic model trains and also had the widest variety of accessories to go with them. Looking through a Lionel train catalog and picking out what you wished you had was fun in itself. Unfortunately, my dream never came true and I had to be satisfied with a Marx-brand train. It wasn't even a close second choice. Instead of Lionel's famous knuckle couplers (like on *real* trains), Marx model trains had some weird-looking couplers that worked nothing at all like the ones connecting actual train cars. After getting over my initial disappointment, I did have some fun building a variety of track layouts which included a set of manually operated switches I later received for my birthday.

Hot-Wheels hadn't been introduced yet, but in my day a boy had a variety of Tootsie-Toys (and other lesser-known brands) he could collect and play with. These were small automobiles, trucks, and military vehicles cast out of cheap metal and painted (usually one solid color). They had steel axles and real rubber tires (which often came off and were lost), but had no fancy, iridescent paint jobs and no flames, racing stripes, spoilers, or any other such exotic features. I received several Tootsie-Toys as gifts through my boyhood years, but back then there weren't nearly as many available as there are Hot-Wheels today.

After the war was over, military toys remained quite popular. I had a small collection of toy soldiers molded from olive drab plastic and posed in various combat positions. But, best of all, I had a windup tank with a cannon in its turret that shot out sparks. The tank was made of stamped metal painted in a camouflage pattern and ran along on rubber tracks that could climb fairly steep inclines. This wasn't a true scale model of any actual tank used in the war, but was sort of a composite design. Actually, it looked more like a WWI tank than one from WWII. A toy tank exactly like the one I had appears very briefly in one of the early scenes in the popular holiday movie *A Christmas Story*. When Ralphie and his little brother are taken downtown by their parents to see the department store Christmas window displays, the tank is seen among other toys as it moves across the bottom of the screen. Look for it next time you watch one of the annual showings of this film classic.

Another toy that I had a lot of fun with was a working model of a clamshell derrick. This toy was over a foot tall, all-metal, and was nicely painted in red and green. It sat on a round base plate that could be rotated 360 degrees with a hand crank. The boom on the derrick could be raised and lowered with another hand crank, and the clamshell bucket could pick up heavy objects and hold them securely. The derrick was an unusual toy; I've never seen another one like it. Sure wish I'd kept it.

After I received a set of scaled-down carpentry tools and a small metal vise one Christmas, my father built me a six-foot long, sturdy, wooden workbench up in my bedroom. I used it frequently to work on all sorts of projects. I asked for and received a number of other full-size tools for Christmas and on my birthday over the following years until I had quite a collection. I still have a few of those tools today. I developed an early desire to have a place for everything and to keep everything in its place. This has stuck with me through the years and has proven to be a good rule.

In addition to these special favorites I've just mentioned, I had a variety of other just plain fun toys including yo-yos, paddle and ball (I was never very good at this), rubber-tipped dart guns, cap guns, a periscope (good for seeing over things or around corners to spy on my sisters), and a really neat pair of Roy Rogers three-power binoculars (these came in handy lots of times).

In those simpler times, we had no computer games. When I was a kid, computers hadn't even been invented yet (at least not ones small enough and affordable enough that people owned their own). There were no PlayStations, no Xboxes, no Wii's, or any of the other electronic gadgets and gizmos that kids play with today for hours on end. But you know what? We still managed to have plenty of fun while we were growing up. We used our imagination and creativity and developed our ability to visualize and construct things. These skills that we sharpened at an early age helped us throughout life in a way that zapping aliens, chasing through mazes and pitfalls, and shooting up cities full of bad guys could never do. And I still wouldn't trade an Erector set for all the computer games in the world.

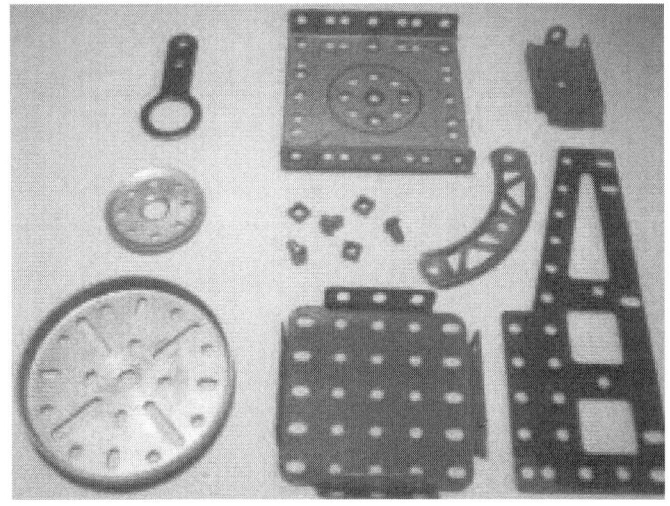

Remnant pieces from my all-metal Buildo set (three on left) and my Erector set (all other odd pieces).

5

Lucky #13

Those who are superstitious about such things might think that pupils attending Horace Mann School were unlucky. Why? Not because they went to classes in one of the oldest elementary school buildings (built in 1873) in the city of Indianapolis, but because their school was stuck with the dreaded number 13—considered by many as the unluckiest of all numbers. We kids who went to P. S. #13 never thought twice about it. We were too young to know much about superstitions, so it didn't matter to us.

While I was in the fourth grade at School #13, something memorable happened that made it the *luckiest* grade school in the entire city. Good fortune came to our school when it was selected (by what method we never knew) from all the others to receive a special visit by none other than Roy Rogers, the so-called "King of the Cowboys." In those days of double features at the movies, one of the films was nearly always a western. And Roy Rogers was the favorite of all the singing cowboys appearing in western movies.

Roy was in town for a big show he was going to put on at the Fairgrounds Coliseum. To help drum up interest in the show, Roy's publicity agent arranged for him to make a free appearance at one—and only one—grade school. And that one lucky school was P. S. #13 because—we heard later—thirteen was Roy's lucky number. I don't remember us being told about his coming in advance; it came as a complete surprise. I sure felt sorry for any kids who were absent from school that day because they missed seeing Roy Rogers live and in person.

The exact date isn't important, but I remember it was a cloudy, cool fall day, probably in September because the leaves were still on the trees. At the appointed time, our teacher, Miss Proctor, said she had a big surprise for us and that we'd be going outside to see something very special. She told us to line up in the cloak hall after putting on our coats, jackets, and sweaters. As we moved from our desks to follow her instructions, all the kids were abuzz about what was happening—especially us boys. This activity was most unusual and we didn't know what was going on.

Each teacher led her class outside to the gravel playground area on the west side of the school building. The teachers arranged us in rows around the outer perimeter, close to the fence. While we stood there looking around and wondering what was happening, we saw Mrs.

Rentschler, our principal, talking to some men we didn't know. She was standing near a microphone. The loudspeaker attached to it looked kind of familiar. In fact, it looked awfully familiar. Wait a minute! There was *my dad* running the sound system. He used it in his show jobs as a professional ventriloquist and magician. What on earth was he doing here? He hadn't said anything to me about being at my school today. I found out later that since Roy's equipment was still packed away on the trucks that traveled with his show and our school didn't have a sound system, Mrs. Rentschler had called my father and asked if the school could borrow his system. Dad and Mom were active in the PTA and he was more than happy to oblige. So, *that's* why he was there that day.

Finally, one of the men stepped up to the microphone and announced in a powerful voice, "Alright, boys and girls, get ready because here comes the one you've been waiting to see, your favorite western hero, Mr. ROY ROGERS!" As he shouted the name and the words boomed out of the speaker, we suddenly heard galloping hooves and gunfire. Then, from around the back corner of the building, here he came. Yes, it really was Roy Rogers riding his famous palomino horse, Trigger, and shooting his pistols. When they reached the center of the playground area, Roy reined Trigger to a quick stop and had him rear up on his hind legs. Roy waved and flashed his big smile. A newspaper photographer snapped a photo at that exact moment. I cut it out of the paper the next day and have saved it all these years. The original is yellowed and faded with age, but it's reproduced at the end of this story.

From the position of my buddy, Ronnie Morris (he's in the front row right behind Trigger's tail and is wearing a long white raincoat), I remember where I was standing in the crowd at the time. I think that's my face just barely peeking over Trigger's rear end. If that's not me, then I'm completely hidden behind his rump. Oh, well. It was a great show anyway. After Roy did several riding and roping tricks, he performed some fancy gun-handling with his six-shooters. The Sons of the Pioneers, Roy's famous musical group, were with him. They sang a couple of old-favorite western songs by themselves and a couple with Roy. Then, all too quickly, the show came to an end.

In his closing remarks, Roy told us to be good students, to mind our teachers and our parents, and to always do our homework. He then asked us, "Will you do that for me, boys and girls?" Of course, we all yelled back our enthusiastic, "YES!" He put his hand up to his ear and said, "I can't hear you, kids. WILL YOU DO THAT FOR ME?" We yelled back even louder than before. Then, he told us good-by and that he'd like to sing one last song before he left. He and the Sons sang his familiar theme song, "Happy Trails to You, Until We Meet Again."

When Roy finished, he took off his big white cowboy hat and waved it over his head. We all cheered and clapped and kept it up until he came back to the mike, said simply, "Thank you. Good-bye." and waved his hat again. Then, we reluctantly followed our teachers back into the school building, hung up our things in the cloak hall, and tried to get back to the business of learning. We all considered ourselves the luckiest kids in the whole city. And, on that one unforgettable day, we were.

Roy Rogers and Trigger during their special unannounced appearance at Public School #13 on September 29, 1948. (originally published in *The Indianapolis News*)

6

Kangaroo Court

> **Kangaroo court: 1** An unauthorized, irregular court, usually disregarding normal legal procedure. **2** Any tribunal in which judgment is rendered arbitrarily or unfairly.
>
> -Webster's Dictionary

Horace Mann Elementary was a good school. I received my second- through fifth-grade education within its ancient brick walls. Many happy memories come to mind whenever I think of School #13. But there's always a dark cloud on the horizon of my memory. And that one cloudy spot was the day I had to appear before the kangaroo court presided over by "Judge" Ruth Wagner.

Ah, Mrs. Wagner. She was fairly young for a teacher in those days when most of them were older and looked like prison matrons. She had reddish hair and an oily face. She wore a lot of red lipstick and had eyes with sort of a wild look in them. Mrs. Wagner looked like someone who got pleasure out of exerting her authority over lesser humans—meaning us kids. You almost expected to see her stalking through the halls of the school with a bullwhip in her hand. Unfortunately, I was to find out firsthand that my opinion of her was quite accurate—except for the part about the bullwhip.

You may be thinking: That's all very interesting, but why would there be a court in an elementary school? Well, there's a reason for everything. And the reason for this so-called court was that Mrs. Wagner was in charge of the traffic patrol boys at School #13. They were stationed at all the busy intersections in the school district to help kids cross the streets safely. These boys also enforced a set of published safety rules that all students were expected to know and obey on their way to and from school. Any violations could be—and usually were—reported to Mrs. Wagner. The only exceptions were in rare cases where the violator might be a good buddy of the traffic boy. In such cases, infractions were sometimes conveniently overlooked for the sake of friendship. At least that was my observation.

Most of my walk to school was along three and a half blocks of Wright Street. I usually obeyed the rules to the letter, but on the day in question I may have thoughtlessly been running to catch up with a friend or might have stepped off the curb to get around a group of other kids. In any case, running and going into the street were both on the official no-no list. I don't remember the name of the traffic boy who reported me, but report me he did. Out of his mouth came those seven dreaded words, "I'm going to turn you in, White."

As a result, on the following Friday when Mrs. Wagner held court in her classroom, I was among those called to appear. I was embarrassed to have to leave my room and for all my classmates to know good and well the reason why. Any students—usually boys—who left their rooms on Friday afternoons were known to be violators going to appear before the dreaded Judge Wagner and her minions. Making my appearance there turned out to be an even worse embarrassment—as I would soon find out.

Each offender was dealt with individually while the rest of us awaited our fate out in the cloak hall (a long narrow area adjacent to a classroom where kids hung their coats). When my turn came and I was called in, I was gripped by fear. I felt like a criminal about to receive the death sentence. Mrs. Wagner was seated at her desk at the front of the classroom. When I entered the back of the room, she looked at me with an evil eye and beckoned me forward with a repeated crooking of her finger. I walked up and stood in front of her desk. She motioned for me to come around to where she was seated and I did so. Then, she pointed toward her lap. I stood there looking at her, momentarily confused. I was in the fourth grade at the time and felt like I was way too big to sit in any woman's lap—especially hers. I shook my head slowly in silent protest. That was a big mistake. She spoke loudly and said, "Young man, get over here." She reached out, grabbed me by my forearms, pulled me towards her, and forcefully sat me in her lap. Then, she wrapped her arms around me. I felt like I was in the clutches of an enraged beast that was about to tear me to shreds—at least verbally.

As I sat there wishing I was somewhere—anywhere—else, I could feel Mrs. Wagner's hot breath in my left ear. Her strong perfume was nauseating and almost gagged me. All the traffic boys were gathered around us in a semicircle and their eyes were riveted on her latest victim—*me*. Mrs. Wagner spoke to me as if I were a small child when she spelled out my offense. The half-circle of onlookers roared with laughter at her manner of speaking and at my obvious discomfort. I don't know if she treated every violator in this demeaning manner, or if it was just something she improvised especially for me. In any case, I didn't like it. I didn't like it at all.

I was so terribly embarrassed and ashamed that I started sniffling. I tried to hold back the tears, but couldn't. As they started trickling down my cheeks, it only made matters worse. Mrs. Wagner mocked me by saying,

"Oh, my. Is the little baby going to cry?" Her phony expression of sympathy did nothing to relieve my discomfort. The boys increased their uproar. She asked me if I was ever going to break another traffic rule and my sincere answer between sniffles was, "Nuh, no, ma'am." And believe me I *meant* it. I never wanted to go through that humiliating experience again. I could only imagine how a second offense would be handled. There were even rumors whispered around school that repeat transgressors received a paddling. That was a sadistic pleasure that I would deny Mrs. Wagner from ever experiencing at the expense of my butt and my dignity.

My behavior along the way to and from school was exemplary from then on. If I spotted a buddy up ahead who I wanted to walk with, I'd yell for him to wait up. No more running or stepping into the street for me. No more violations. No more appearances before Judge Wagner's kangaroo court.

Front entrance into Public School #13 as it looks today—nearly the same as it looked back in the late 1940s when I was a student there. The old school building was converted into modern condominiums several years ago. The bronze plaque on right identifies it as being on the National Registry of Historic Places.

My parents arranged for my sister, Sandy, and me to transfer from School #13 to School #18 after I completed the fifth grade. This was primarily because they wanted to spare us the long walk to School #8 where #13 graduates went next. I don't think my traumatic day in traffic court had anything to do with it because I never told my folks about it. But, in any case, I never had to face Mrs. Wagner in her position as a sixth-grade teacher. I felt like I'd cheated the hangman and was glad to escape any further exposure to the tender mercies of dear Mrs. Wagner. All kidding aside, I'm actually grateful to her for helping to instill in me a deep respect for all laws by demonstrating the dire consequences of violating them.

7

The Great Backyard Chicken Slaughter

The Duncans lived across the alley from our house on Wright Street. This family was a dad and mom, plus three children a few years younger than my sisters and me. Because of the age difference, we never played with their kids. The Duncans stayed on their side of the alley and we stayed on our side. Although we didn't live during economic hard times like during a depression, people in those days were frugal and looked for ways to save money. Mrs. Duncan must have discovered that it was a little cheaper to buy a *live* chicken at the Fountain Square Poultry Market on Virginia Avenue and not pay extra for a "dressed" one that had been killed, plucked, and cleaned.

Anyway, an old wooden cage containing a large white chicken appeared one day in the Duncan's backyard. Sandy, Jackie, and I noticed it sitting out by the former livery stable building that occupied the back half of their lot. The caged chicken stayed there a few days and we had almost forgotten about it. That is, until late one afternoon when we noticed unusual activity over in the Duncan's backyard. A small group had gathered, including Mrs. Duncan and her kids, plus another lady and a couple of other small children. The woman might have been Mrs. Duncan's sister or a friend who came to assist her in what she was about to do. And what she was about to do was kill the unfortunate chicken for supper. Why she wanted to perform this gruesome task in front of a bunch of innocent young children is beyond me. But there they were, all standing around waiting for the big show to begin.

My sisters and I were out in our backyard and we, too, could sense that something out of the ordinary was about to happen across the alley. Our yard was enclosed by a chain link fence and the Duncan's yard was fenced with narrow wooden boards separated by wide gaps. So, we had no trouble seeing the action as it took place. It began with Mrs. Duncan and her friend discussing their plan of attack. Her friend then went to the cage and after several attempts grabbed the condemned chicken by its legs. As she fought to keep her hold on the bird and carry it across the yard to Mrs. Duncan it was frantically flapping its wings as if it knew it had only seconds to live. This started a wave of excitement among the children watching. The chicken nearly got loose, but the woman held on for dear life.

Evidently the Duncans didn't own an axe or a hatchet to behead the chicken, and they had no chopping block on which to do it. Instead of the traditional killing method, Mrs. Duncan or her friend could have used the alternative of holding the chicken by its head and giving it a quick twist in order to break its neck. They either didn't know about this trick, or were too squeamish to perform it. So, instead of using either of these tried-and-true methods, Mrs. Duncan had decided to use a large butcher knife to sever the chicken's head.

This may have seemed like a reasonable alternative to the axe or hatchet, but without a chopping block it was doomed to failure. As her friend held on to the still-flopping fowl, Mrs. Duncan took a healthy swing at it with the knife. She missed, then tried again. As you can imagine, it was *not* a quick, clean kill. In fact, she only partly severed the head. And, of course, when you cut a chicken's throat it immediately starts spurting blood. The friend suddenly was holding not only a thrashing chicken but one that was gushing blood as well. She did what any woman would do—she screamed and let go of it.

Well, the chicken hit the ground running with its head flopping up and down against its breast while leading the two ladies on a wild chase around the confines of the yard. The kids were all screaming and scampering in every direction. Mrs. Duncan was right behind the wounded chicken swinging at it with the butcher knife every chance she got. It's a wonder she didn't slash some of the kids in all the chaos. The half-decapitated chicken couldn't see where it was going, of course, and the poor thing kept running into the fence and any other solid object it encountered. My sisters and I almost rolled on the ground laughing at the unbelievable spectacle taking place. It was funny in a way that only something that shouldn't be amusing in the least unexpectedly turns out to be hilarious.

We couldn't see exactly what happened next, but the chicken either bled to death and gave up running for its life or Mrs. Duncan caught up with it and gave it the coup de grace. In any case, the chicken was finally dead. We could see it lying there in the yard in the middle of a circle of suddenly silent onlookers.

While we all watched, Mrs. Duncan approached the now lifeless carcass and prodded it with the knife just to make sure the thing was truly dead. Next, she finished removing the dangling head. She didn't have to worry about bleeding the carcass since the chicken's dying exertion had evidently pumped it dry. Then, she triumphantly carried the now headless chicken through the back door and into their house. All the kids and the other lady followed the victory parade led by Mrs. Duncan and disappeared inside. The show was over as quickly as it had begun.

Now that the commotion had ended, our laughter died down. My sisters and I ran inside still snickering to tell our mother about what we'd just witnessed. Since I was the oldest, I told the story to Mom while Sandy and Jackie filled in with additional details. She could hardly believe our description of the event.

The Duncans wisely never tried to save money in this way again. So, The Great Backyard Chicken Slaughter was a one-time-only event. Without a doubt, it was the most exciting thing that happened on Wright Street that entire summer. My sisters and I still laugh about it.

My sister Sandy told me after I wrote this story that she thought the Duncan's chicken came from a different source. According to her, the Duncan kids had each received a baby chick for Easter (G. C. Murphy's Five & Dime sold them) and they had grown into full-size chickens, one of which suffered the terrible fate described above. She could be right. If so, I don't remember or know for sure what happened to the other two chickens. Maybe they flew the coop.

8

An Ingenious Solution to An Unusual Problem

During World War II all the automobile companies were converted from producing cars for civilians to making weapons of war for the armed forces of America and her allies. As soon as possible after the war was won, these companies switched back to producing motor vehicles for the general public. Due to the great demand, there was a long waiting list to purchase certain popular makes and models of cars. Some people didn't want to wait and bought less-popular vehicles that were their second or third choice.

And so it was that one evening after work, Dad came home driving a big, ugly, two-tone green 1947 Nash Ambassador four-door sedan. He'd traded in our old 1940 Studebaker Champion sedan in order to purchase the Nash. After he pulled up and parked in front of our house on Wright Street, some of the neighbors came over to look at the car. Buying a new automobile in those days was an occasion to take note of. This was Dad's first brand-new car and he was mighty proud of it.

Dad pointed out the Ambassador's wide white-wall tires, its fancy radio with push buttons, and an accessory not all cars had: a big chrome spotlight mounted on the driver's-side door pillar. I'd thought that only police cruisers had such lights, but our car came with one. The auto factories loaded their cars with lots of accessories in those post-war days when new vehicles were still scarce and the eager buyers snapped them up whether they wanted all the extras or not.

Dad worked for *The Indianapolis News* and one of his many responsibilities was to make sure that any missed customers in his district were taken a paper. He said the spotlight would be a big help when looking for the addresses of such people, especially during the late fall and winter when darkness came early. Later, after dark, Dad played around with the spotlight's control handle inside the car and used it to direct the light in any desired direction. He demonstrated the light's powerful beam and lit up houses four blocks away. I didn't care much for the car itself, but I thought the spotlight was really neat.

Our family gulped down supper in great excitement as we all talked about our new car. As soon as the girls cleared the table and Mom rinsed off the dishes, it was time to take a ride. As we all piled into the car, a bit of a fuss developed. Each of us kids wanted to sit by a window; but, like any car, the back seat had only two side windows. This hadn't been much of a problem in the old Studebaker, but now that he had a brand-new car, suddenly the window seats were much more desirable. Mom settled our disagreement by telling us we would take turns each time we rode in the car. Sandy and I each got a window on the first ride with Jackie sitting in the middle straddling the hump.

Dad drove down Shelby Street as far south as Garfield Park. After looping through the park and taking us over Tickle-Belly Bridge, he headed up South East Street. Turning east on Morris, he followed it over to the alley running down to our garage. When we arrived at the intersection of the two alleys at the back corner of our lot, all of us except Dad got out of the car. I performed my regular duty of opening the garage doors, swinging them back, and fastening them in place. Mom and the girls went on in through the garage and headed across the backyard to the house.

As Dad began maneuvering the big Ambassador into our garage, it was obvious to me—and I'm sure to him as well—that the new Nash was considerably larger than our old Studebaker, both in width and length. He was as careful as only a new car owner can be and succeeded in lining the Nash up and pulling it inside the garage. There was only one problem. When I went back to swing the garage doors closed, I immediately noticed that a good two feet of the Nash's tail end was sticking outside the garage. There was no way the garage doors could be closed and latched.

Dad climbed out of the car and came back to see why I hadn't closed the doors like I usually did. He saw the problem and quickly came up with a temporary solution. He told me to run to the house and get him a coat hanger. When I brought one back, he untwisted it. Then, stepping outside the garage, we swung the doors closed as far as they'd go. There was still a wide gap between them. Dad took the coat hanger wire and used it to hold the doors in place by looping each end through the latching hasp hardware on the doors. Of course, this provided absolutely no security, but in those days that wasn't so much of a concern. We then walked down the alley and entered our backyard by the side gate.

A couple days later when it was Saturday and I was around to help him, Dad figured out a permanent solution to our "short garage" problem. On the nose end of the garage building was a room we used for a tool shed. His plan was to cut out a large rectangular section of the end wall of the garage and let the nose of the Nash stick into the shed. I had to hand it to my father, this was the perfect solution. In order to protect our new car from any potential damage, he said we'd build a housing over its front end. We had several old wooden doors stored in the shed and these would form the walls and roof of the housing. Dad and I drove to Forbes Lumber over on Kentucky Avenue and picked up some two-by-fours and nails. When Mom wasn't with us and it was just Dad and me, I got to ride shotgun. I felt like hot stuff riding up front in our new car—even though it was an ugly two-tone green Nash.

After buying the lumber, Dad pulled an old blanket out of the trunk. We spread the blanket on the roof to protect the paint. Next, we carefully laid each two-by-four on the blanket. After they were all in place, Dad wrapped the blanket over the boards and tied their ends into a bundle with some sash cord he'd brought along. Then, we ran cord from the ends of the board bundle to the front and rear bumpers and tied the load down securely. Dad may never have been a Boy Scout or a sailor, but he sure knew how to tie good knots. We drove home slowly and avoided any bumps so the lumber wouldn't slide off the roof sideways. After making it home safely from the lumberyard, we were again very careful as we unloaded the wood from the car roof and carried it out into the backyard.

I helped Dad measure the width of the Nash and the height of its hood (which unlike today's cars was nearly a foot higher than the fenders). He added six inches on each side.

Then, we measured out and marked the width and height of the rectangular area we would cut out of the wall. Dad made sure we double-checked all our measurements before we started cutting. He said the old rule of "measure twice, cut once; measure once, cut twice" was a good one to follow. Anytime I've carelessly broken that rule in the years since, I've regretted it.

Now, the real work began. There were no power saws in those days. At least Dad didn't own one if there were. So, we got to do all the cutting the hard way: by hand. Our old carpenter's saw was probably way overdue for sharpening, but we used it anyway. Dad would cut awhile and then while he rested, I'd cut awhile. Then, I'd take a rest while he resumed sawing. The wood used in the dividing wall between the garage and the shed was thick and hard. It must have taken us an hour just to cut out the opening. Boy, were my arms aching. Dad's probably were, too, but he didn't say anything.

After we sanded off the rough edges and splinters, Dad decided to give the new opening a try. He nosed the car all the way into the garage to make sure the opening we'd cut was adequate. It was. Our garage (which had originally been used to store a buggy) was so old that it had a packed dirt floor. The shed (which had originally been used as a horse stall) had a concrete floor. After making the opening in the wall, the edge of the now exposed concrete shed floor made a perfect stop block to keep from driving the car in too far and bumping the enclosure we were about to build.

We took a lunch break and then went back to work. Several hours later, just before supper time, our project was completed. We stood back and admired our handiwork. The protective enclosure in the shed wasn't pretty, but it was functional. Now, when Dad pulled the Ambassador into the garage, the nose was protected, and the garage doors closed and latched properly. The housing we constructed in the shed was so strong and well-built that we could use the top of it for storage. We may have lost a considerable volume of space in the shed, but we ended up using the top of the housing to store all the screens from our front porch. This had the side benefit of keeping them up out of harm's way during the off-season.

My father's ingenious solution to this unusual problem served as a memorable lesson in developing my own creative thinking process. This was one of many such lessons learned during my "on-the-job" training while growing up. These lessons helped to mold me into the person I am today. And it was partly because Dad couldn't fit our big new car into our little old garage out behind our house on Wright Street.

When the Indiana State Highway Department was buying up property in our neighborhood that was within the proposed right-of-way for the new interstate highways being built in the 1960s, they bought our house at 1218 Wright Street. But because the right-of-way cut across our lot at an angle, only the house and the front portion of our lot were purchased. Our garage and an odd-shaped piece of the backyard were not acquired by the state. My mother was a widow by then and sold the garage and land to our neighbors behind us. They used the garage for storage another thirty years until time and the elements finally took their toll and our old garage was torn down. Only the concrete foundation remains today.

9

Mystery in the Night Sky

On a summer night that seemed no different from any other in 1949, I saw something truly mysterious in the sky over Indianapolis. I was about ten-and-a-half-years-old at the time. As I began climbing the dark stairway to my bedroom that night, I came to the landing where the stairs made a left turn. There was a two-foot square, swing-in window above the landing. The window was wide open since the weather was hot and home air-conditioning was still years in the future.

As my head came even with the window sill, something drew my attention upward into the night sky. Strange, almost ghostly looking, pale-bluish lights tinged with some soft red shimmered high above the city. The pattern of the lights reminded me of colossal draperies moving in slow motion as if stirred and rippled by a soft breeze. I'd never seen anything like it before—nor have I seen anything like it since. And I don't mind telling you, seeing those lights as a kid gave me the willies.

I stood there looking up into the sky for a

couple of minutes in boyish fascination mixed with a tad of fear. I remember thinking, *This sure can't be anything manmade. There must be a God to make something this big and beautiful.* The unearthly, colorful lights in the sky were the most wondrous aerial sight I'd ever seen, even more awe-inspiring than the rare double rainbow I'd witnessed earlier that same summer. Since I had absolutely no idea what these weird lights were, I quickly went and found Dad. He and Mom were sitting out on the front porch. They were surprised to see me and wondered why I was still up since I'd supposedly gone to bed several minutes earlier. I told them about seeing the strange lights in the sky. The three of us looked off the porch toward the north, but our view was partly blocked by the roof of the house across the alley.

At my urging, Dad followed me back to the stairway window. When we arrived, I said, "Look up there. Can you see it?" All he said in response, was a simple, "Yes," in a hushed voice. We stood there side-by-side on the dark stairs, mesmerized for a minute or two in total silence as we watched the eerie light patterns ripple across the sky. Finally, I said, almost in a whisper, "What is it, Dad?" He explained that what we were seeing was something called the northern lights. They weren't usually visible this far south, he said, so that night was a truly rare occurrence. He wasn't sure of the details about what produced these patterns of light high up in the atmosphere, but thought it had something to do with radiation from the sun. He was as amazed to see them as I was and told me he'd never seen them before during his entire lifetime (he was then about thirty-six).

My sisters were already in bed, so Dad didn't rouse them out to see the strange lights. I figured since they were girls, they probably wouldn't have been that excited about seeing them anyway. When I told Sandy and Jackie the next morning about what I'd seen the night before, they were mildly curious, but expressed no real regret at having missed this maybe-once-in-a-lifetime opportunity to see the northern lights. I guess girls back then just weren't as scientifically minded as boys were.

That afternoon when the newspaper came it reported on the local appearance of the northern lights. There was a big front-page article about them which interviewed some top astronomer. Among other details, he said that the lights' scientific name was the *aurora borealis.* (I've always liked the way those two words sound when you say them.) The radio also ran news reports about the lights and confirmed what Dad had said about their visibility over Indianapolis being quite an unusual event. They're normally visible only much further north in Canada and other areas near the Arctic Circle.

After seeing the newspaper article, my sisters decided to join me in looking for the lights the next night. Unfortunately, it was cloudy and—if they were still up there—they weren't visible. The night after that was clear, but the northern lights were gone by then. So, the girls missed their big chance to see what only I'd been privileged to witness.

After I went to bed that night and lay there thinking before going to sleep, I realized just how lucky I was. If I'd been in more of a hurry, or hadn't happened to glance out the window on the way up to my room, I would've missed my once-in-a-lifetime opportunity to see the unforgettable northern lights on that one-and-only night they were visible in the skies over Indianapolis.

As a result of this singular experience, I learned at an early age to always be aware of my surroundings. You just never know what you might miss if you don't stay alert and keep your eyes open.

10

Not in the Script

Back in the days before school boards banned prayer, the display of the Ten Commandments, and any reference to Christian holidays, most elementary schools routinely presented an annual Christmas program. When I was in the fifth grade at Horace Mann School #13, we performed the well-known "A Christmas Carol," that classic story by Charles Dickens about Ebenezer Scrooge and how he is visited by three ghosts on Christmas Eve which results in his rediscovering the joy of celebrating Christmas.

I remember nothing at all about how the play was cast, but somehow I ended up with the role of Bob Cratchit. A buddy of mine, Frank Coulter (who was kind of small for his age), was given the role of Tiny Tim. I never thought of myself as an actor and memorizing lines was a real chore for a kid my age—especially a boy with little or no desire to get up and perform in front of people. Our production was a much-shortened version of the Dickens classic, so our dialogue was simplified and reduced to a minimum. And was I glad of that.

On the night of our program, the school's auditorium on the second floor was packed full. The parents of every child in the play were there to see how well their sons and daughters performed. I was nervous, as were most of the kids, and afraid I'd muff my lines in front of my folks. To cover that very real possibility, one of the teachers acted as a prompter and stood off to one side behind the curtain with a copy of the script. If any of us went blank—and some of us did—she'd read the start of our line to us without speaking it loudly enough for the audience to hear. There were several of these long, awkward pauses while stymied actors and actresses looked up at the ceiling and tried vainly to remember their lines. The prompter repeated them in ever louder whispers until the dialogue started flowing once again and the play continued.

The auditorium we were performing in had been constructed by removing a wall between two classrooms and combining them into one large open area. The old cloak hall for one of the former classrooms was located immediately behind the stage. Shelves had been built along one wall on which a hodgepodge of items were stored. A small sink had been installed in one corner where the ladies would wash the dishes used in serving refreshments at PTA meetings and other special activities. On a shelf over the sink sat a box of soap powder; the brand name in white letters on the dark-blue box was Ivory Snow (remember that name).

While Frank and I were standing near the sink awaiting our cue to go onstage, I looked over and noticed the soap box. The brand name jumped out at me—especially that word Snow—and instantly gave me an idea which I thought at the time was quite clever. I said, "Hey, Frank. Let's take some of this stuff and sprinkle it on our hats and coats, so when we go on stage it'll look like we've really just come in out of a snowstorm." Frank thought it was a great idea. So, just before we went onstage, I shook some of the powder out of the box and onto both our heads and shoulders. Then, deciding it wasn't quite enough, I sprinkled on even more. We entered the backstage area from the cloakroom just before the teacher directing the play motioned for us to go on. If she noticed the white powder all over us, she didn't have time to say anything about it as she gave us our cue.

At this point in the play, Mr. Cratchit had to carry Tiny Tim on stage into a scene set in the parlor of their home. I was just a skinny kid and Frank Coulter may have been small for his age, but he certainly wasn't tiny. On cue, I quickly bent down, picked up Frank and his wooden crutch, and lugged him in my arms out to center stage. As I did, his nose was just above my shoulder and he must have inhaled a good snoot full of the powdered soap. His reaction to it was as loud as it was unexpected and he went into a sudden fit of sneezing. Each sneeze was louder than the last. It startled me and I nearly dropped him. At the same time the audience began laughing.

"A Christmas Carol" wasn't meant to be a comedy, but it turned into one for a few moments. As Frank sneezed, he shook me and more soap powder flew up into his face starting the cycle all over again. His continued sneezing and the audience's increasing laughter were obviously not in the script. As a result, none of us on stage knew what to do or say. Even if we had, we wouldn't have been heard because of Frank's loud sneezing and the audience's even louder reaction. The girl playing my wife and I just stood there looking at each another anxiously. The prompter must have been momentarily confused too because no cues were forthcoming—at least none that we could hear.

Finally, Frank's sneezing fit subsided and out of desperation, I ad-libbed, "Sounds like you're coming down with a really bad cold, Tiny Tim." The audience just roared. The girl playing Mrs. Cratchit picked up her line from there and the play continued without any further hitches.

The Christmas play we presented that night was a big hit with the appreciative audience. But Frank's sneezing spell and my well-timed ad-lib were all that most people were talking about as the cast circulated among the parents and the other children afterward. While we all lined up for punch and homemade Christmas cookies, some adults wise-cracked to Frank, "Hope you get over your cold, Tiny Tim." Frank and I just grinned, rolled our eyes at one another, and shook our heads.

We were afraid that we'd be in trouble for our impromptu use of the Ivory Snow and for disrupting the seriousness of the story. Instead, Mrs. Rentschler, the school principal, complimented us for our cleverness and for adding a well-received moment of levity to the school's annual Christmas play. We sure hadn't planned it that way, but it did turn out pretty darn funny.

11

Something New Called Television

No matter in what era, there have always been some people who enjoy being on the cutting edge of technology, especially in the field of consumer electronics. Others are not so concerned. Back during the 1940s, my parents were perfectly happy and satisfied with the entertainment and news provided by our trusty old radio. In those days every home had one; many had more than one.

The radio provided hours of soap operas in the afternoons for stay-at-home moms (which most of them were), children's programs in the late afternoon (after kids were home from school) and on Saturdays, comedy and drama shows in the evening, and musical programs featuring popular big bands and famous singers of the day.

When my folks bought a new radio, I was fortunate to inherit the old one: a table-model, Detrola-brand multiband. It had a large illuminated dial listing all the options available. By carefully turning one of the three knobs you could pick up all sorts of unusual and exciting programs and voices coming across the airwaves. These included local and national radio stations, plus police and fire department communications, shortwave broadcasts, and foreign language programs. The radio came with a long antenna wire that I stretched across my bedroom to enhance reception. I was fascinated by the great variety of places and things I could pick up on the radio.

Our new family radio was a sleek Crosley with a dark-maroon plastic cabinet in the classic Art Deco style and had pushbuttons that could be set for favorite stations. The old Detrola in its rustic wooden cabinet looked rather outdated in comparison. But it still worked fine and I enjoyed listening to it for several years while a teenager.

All was well in the White house until something happened across the street. The Many (pronounced "man-E") family, who lived diagonally from us on the other side of Wright Street were the first family in our block—and probably one of the first in our entire neighborhood—to buy the latest and greatest thing to come along since radio. It was something new called *television*. The Manys were the focus of everyone's curiosity and most people's envy. Kids from along our block would actually go up on the Many's front porch and stand there looking in through their living room windows just to catch a glimpse of the mysterious box that had both sound and a moving picture. I know because my two sisters and I were among them. Since Carol Many was the age of my sister, Sandy, and they were occasional playmates, she invited us in for a better look. The powerful allure of television was so strong that we snuck across the street and went inside the Many's without prior permission from our parents. This was a double major violation of "the rules" at the White house.

Now, remember, we aren't talking about big-screen, high-definition TV. In fact, back then the first television screens were *round* and only about a foot in diameter. Watching a picture on such a screen was something like looking through a porthole on a ship. The picture, of course, was only in black-and-white, and rather grainy. A V-shaped so-called "rabbit ears" antenna sat atop the cabinet and Mr. Many would tinker with it to get the best picture to come in when he changed channels.

I still remember the very first television program I ever saw at their house: a popular puppet show called *Howdy Doody* starring a freckle-faced marionette by that name. He interacted with a live man named Buffalo Bob who was dressed in sort of a western outfit complete with a fringed buckskin coat. A clown on the show was named Clarabelle, which seemed like an odd name for a *male* clown. An American Indian girl named Princess Summer-Spring-

Winter-Fall also appeared from time to time. It wasn't much of a show, but it was television. We were so enthralled we would've watched anything.

My sisters and I went home and raved about the marvelous new thing we'd seen over at the Manys. Our excited comments betrayed the fact that we had been somewhere we shouldn't have. Our father was more concerned about our breaking the rules and what our punishment would be for going over there without asking permission than he was about what we'd seen and heard. He not only wasn't impressed, he didn't even seem interested. Dad said he was going to wait and see if this television thing really caught on or if it was just a temporary fad that would soon die out. In the meantime, we continued listening to the radio as we had for years previously. As the months went by, however, it became more and more obvious that TV was here to stay. And the innovations kept coming.

In order to keep up with the latest available technology, the Manys soon added an accessory to their TV set. This was a large magnifying glass on a frame that was mounted in front of the screen to increase its size. The only problem was that the magnifier also increased the distortions around the edges. If you sat directly in front of the television screen, the effect was not too noticeable. But if you sat over on either side, people on the screen looked pretty weird—like in a fun house mirror and kind of blurry.

The next thing we knew, the Manys had traded in their porthole model for a newer set with a semi-rectangular screen. The corners of the picture had large radiuses and the four sides of the screen weren't straight, but were slightly curved. It wasn't at all like the perfectly rectangular, picture-frame screens of today, but it was a giant leap forward at the time.

Shortly after that, the Manys added yet another new feature. This was a large sheet of plastic that covered the TV screen in a crude attempt to create what passed for "color television." The top third of the overlay was tinted blue, the center band was sort of a tan color, and the bottom third was green. I guess the idea was to give the sky in scenic shots a blue look and provide a skin tone for close-ups of people. I don't know about the green. I think it was there to add more color, but never seemed appropriate unless the scene showed a lawn or a grassy field. Needless to say, most of the time these three colors were totally inappropriate for whatever was on the screen. These color overlays never caught on with TV set owners and died a quick death years before true color television was finally introduced.

A year or so later, after most everyone else on our block had joined the latest trend and bought television sets, our folks finally gave in and joined them. Dad bought a new Crosley floor model television and had it delivered to our house. Boy, were we kids all excited. TV was even better than Christmas—because it was available every day, not just once a year. Our set had about a 16-inch screen and a 10-inch speaker below it mounted behind a woven fabric covering.

Of course, in those early days of television there was no such thing as a remote control. Dad didn't need one; he had *me*. Whenever he wanted the channel changed to another of the three available, he would just tell me and I'd go do it for him. As my sisters grew older, they, too, were entrusted with this sacred duty. Then, we had to take turns twisting the big channel selector dial under the right-hand corner of the screen. What a privilege we felt was ours to be so entrusted.

Dad started out using rabbit ears, but soon had a large aluminum antenna mounted up on the roof. It looked like the frame of a box kite with extra angled pieces attached and sticking out in various directions. A coaxial wire ran down from the antenna and connected to the back of our TV set (this was the only television "cable" we ever knew about in those days). Having an antenna on your roof was a status symbol back then and we were proud to have one. Later, motor-driven, rotating antennas became available, but Dad stuck with the one we had. He said it was plenty good enough.

Programming in the early days of television was extremely limited. Even though Indianapolis was a sizable city, it had only three channels—one for each of the major networks. Soon a fourth independent local channel was added. Programs weren't available 24 hours a day. And at first there was no *TV Guide* or schedules in the newspaper to let viewers know what programs were going to be aired. Most programs were live and many amusing flubs were shown as they actually happened. Stage hands accidentally walking in front of the TV camera were the most common. Falling props and pieces of scenery also occurred without warning from time to time.

Occasionally, during the hours when no regular programs were showing, the TV stations ran brief films of well-known songs featuring music, dancing, and elaborate scenery and costumes. I guess these were the forerunner of what later became music videos. We were so fascinated by the marvel of television that we'd eagerly watch just about anything they put on the screen. Even the commercials were fascinating. Many featured dancing products, puppets, or animation to promote their sponsors. Listening to the radio almost became a thing of the past; however, I still listened to the latest hit music while doing homework up in my room.

At first, only a few hours of TV programming were available each day, mainly late in the afternoon and during the evening. The rest of the time the TV screen was filled with what was called a test pattern. This was a layout of lines, letters, numbers, and various blocks of black and gray tones. Oh, yes, there was also a small picture of an Indian chief wearing a full-feathered war bonnet. The purpose of all this was to help early TV owners fine-tune their sets. Other signs that we often saw were ones reading Technical Difficulties and Please Stand By. The picture would disappear for awhile and the station would just broadcast music until the problem was fixed. Sometimes, it took them quite a while. But we sat there waiting patiently no matter how long it took. If you stayed up late enough at night (which we seldom ever got to do at our age), you'd see each station sign off at midnight with the playing of the National Anthem while a picture of a fluttering American flag was shown.

Common problems faced by viewers in the early days of television were: the appearance of a "snowy" picture (looked like you were watching it through a snow storm); an out-of-synch picture that broke up into a series of diagonal bands in various shades of black, white, and gray; and a rolling picture which kept moving up across the screen—sometimes slowly, sometimes fast. These and other problems required frequent visits by a TV repairman to replace tubes (this was back before solid-state circuitry was invented) and to tinker with various adjustments. Some of these guys were honest and some were not-so-honest. It was hard to tell the difference when their specialized services were almost like performing magic in the eyes of the general public.

Doctors making house calls were nearly a thing of the past when I was kid. But because television sets at first were mostly floor models in bulky, heavy cabinets, TV repairmen came to your home. And their arrival was awaited as anxiously as any doctor ever was. The worst thing you could hear the TV guy say was, “I’m going to have to take it into the shop.” The man would then go in through the back of the cabinet and perform something like major surgery by pulling out the entire guts of the set and hauling them away. In some cases, if Dad was home when the man came, he would help the guy carry our entire set out to his panel truck or station wagon and load it into the back. It was like seeing a family member put into an ambulance and hauled off to the hospital. Then, we had to suffer through several agonizing days of no TV to watch. We’d go back to just plain old radio for awhile. But the radio lacked the appeal it held before the days of television. When our TV set was finally returned, it was a time of great rejoicing.

The television set quickly took the place

of the traditional family hearth as a focal point for family gatherings. Many fond memories come to mind of sitting around the living room together with my two sisters and our parents, five pairs of eyes glued to the TV screen. During the commercial breaks (which weren't nearly as frequent as they are today) we'd sometimes make comments and discuss various aspects of the program being watched. During the week, we had to have our homework completed before we were allowed to watch any TV—talk about a motivating incentive. Our bedtime was nine o'clock on school nights (including Sundays) and ten on the weekends. So, our daily exposure to television was strictly limited. My sisters and I really looked forward to Saturdays because there were lots of TV shows aimed just at kids. Advertisers quickly learned the importance of targeting children who would get their parents to spend money on the products featured in TV commercials.

Some television programs I remember watching and enjoying include:

ADVENTURE – I Led Three Lives . . . Ramar of the Jungle . . . Sky King . . . Space Patrol . . . Tom Corbett, Space Cadet.

COMEDY – Amos & Andy (first all-black TV show—remember Kingfish?) . . . Burns & Allen Show . . . Edgar Bergen & Charlie McCarthy

Show (a not-so-good ventriloquist who was nevertheless quite popular) . . . Ernie Kovacs Comedy Specials (really offbeat and featuring his lovely wife, singer Edie Adams) . . . Gary Moore Show (remember his sidekick Durwood Kirby? He was from Indianapolis and went to Tech) . . . I Love Lucy . . . Jackie Gleason Show . . . Ken Murry Show . . . Milton Berle Show . . . Ozzie & Harriet . . . Phil Silvers Show . . . Red Skelton Show . . . Stu Erwin Show (remember Willie the handyman?).

DRAMA - Kraft Television Theater . . . Lux Video Theater . . . Playhouse 90.

COWBOYS / WESTERNS - Bat Masterson (starred Gene Barry) . . . Daniel Boone . . . Death Valley Days (hosted originally by "The Old Ranger" and later by none other than Ronald Reagan, our future president) . . . Gene Autry Show . . . Gunsmoke (starred James Arness as Sheriff Matt Dillon and his deputy Chester, played by Dennis Weaver) . . . Have Gun, Will Travel (starred Richard Boone as Paladin) . . . Hopalong Cassidy (starred William Boyd) . . . Rawhide (starred a young Clint Eastwood before he made his string of famous "spaghetti westerns") . . . Roy Rogers & Dale Evans Show . . . The Adventures of Davy Crockett, King of the Wild Frontier (starred Fess Parker wearing his trademark coonskin cap) . . . The Cisco Kid (starred Duncan Reynaldo and his sidekick Pancho, played by Leo Carillo) . . . The Lone Ranger (starred Clinton Moore and his "faithful Indian companion" Tonto, played by Jay Silverheels) . . . The Rifleman (starred Chuck Connery) . . . Wagon Train (starred Ward Bond) . . . Wanted Dead or Alive (starred Steve McQueen before he hit the big time) . . . Wild Bill Hickok (starred Guy Madison and his sidekick Jingles, played by Andy Devine).

GAME SHOWS – Beat the Clock (hosted by Bud Collier) . . . I've Got A Secret . . . Name that Tune . . . You Bet Your Life . . . 20 Questions.

HISTORY/DOCUMENTARIES – Air Power . . . Crusade in Europe . . . Men of Annapolis . . . Navy Log . . . See It Now . . . The Silent Service (about submarines in World War II) . . . The 20th Century . . . Victory at Sea . . . West Point Stories.

KIDS – Howdy Doody Time . . . Kukla, Fran, & Ollie (Fran was a woman, the other two were hand puppets) . . . Super Circus (starred the beautiful blonde majorette, Mary Hartline; a ringmaster named Claude Kirchner, and three clowns—Cliffy, little Scampy, and Nicky, who looked like a hobo) . . . Wonderful World of Disney.

MUSIC – Billy Rose Show . . . Dinah Shore Show . . . Fred Waring and the Pennsylvanians . . . Mitch Miller Show . . . Nat King Cole Show . . . Paul Whiteman Show . . . Perry Como Show . . . Spike Jones Show (wacky music and comedy) . . . Ted Lewis Show . . . Tommy & Jimmy Dorsey Show . . . Your Hit Parade.

NEWS – Douglas Edwards and the News . . . Edward R. Murrow and the Nightly News . . . John Cameron Swayze.

POLICE / DETECTIVE – Big Town . . . Boston Blackie (starred Kent Taylor) . . . Dragnet (starred Jack Webb) . . . Highway Patrol (starred Broderick Crawford) . . . Rocky King, Detective . . . Streets of San Francisco.

SPORTS – Professional Wrestling (locally produced program featuring matches between big name wrestlers) . . . Roller Derby . . .Wednesday Night Fights (sponsored by Pabst Blue Ribbon Beer and Gillette razors).

VARIETY – Arthur Godfrey Show . . . Arthur Godfrey's Talent Scouts . . . Cavalcade of Stars . . . Ted Mack's Original Amateur Hour . . . Toast of the Town with Ed Sullivan (later called The Ed Sullivan Show) . . . Your Show of Shows.

This was television in the late 1940s and

early '50s. And it all started with a TV set having a 12-inch porthole-shaped screen. Things were never again the same on Wright Street—or anywhere else across America. Television was here to stay.

One of several websites to check out for more memories about the early days of television is **www.skooldays.com** It has several categories of memories grouped by each decade clear back to 1900. This is a real fun site to visit.

12

Olive Branch

Occasionally, we still sing that old hymn "This is My Father's World" at the church where my wife and I are members. Whenever I hear those familiar words, my mind flies back through the years and across the miles to a two-story, red brick building on the corner of Raymond and South Pennsylvania streets. The sign in front identifies it as the Olive Branch Christian Church. After we moved to Wright Street, our parents took my two sisters and me to church and Sunday School at Olive Branch every week when we were kids. There was no debate about whether or not we would go, we just went. Going to church was a regular part of our family's Sundays and we actually looked forward to attending. We kids had our neighborhood friends, our school friends, and on Sundays we got to spend time with our church friends.

One of the main reasons I enjoyed going to Olive Branch as a youngster was that they had a program called Junior Church for kids ages nine through eleven. Children younger than that went to a similar program called Primary Church for six through eight-year-olds. When we reached age twelve we graduated to "big church" as we called it. Then, we could participate in the adult worship services with our parents. By that time we knew and understood to some degree what was going on, why it was happening, and how we were expected to behave.

Junior Church was led by a wonderful middle-aged couple named Emory and Fanchon Eaton. He was a lanky six-footer with glasses and almost no hair, who always wore polka dot bow ties. She was short and stout, wore glasses, and had gray hair. They both smiled a lot and always seemed happy to see us rag-tag assortment of young heathens who descended upon them every Sunday. They were assisted by Mrs. Ruark, who played the piano while we learned and sang "Jesus Loves Me" and a variety of other hymns and gospel songs. She was a sturdily built, tall woman who wore her whitish-gray hair coiled in a bun on the back of her head. Her eyeglasses had thick, black frames holding large round lenses, which gave her sort of an owlish look. She usually had a jaunty hat of some kind perched atop her head. Back in those days, it was the custom for all women to wear hats and white gloves to church. Mrs. Ruark skipped the gloves since she played the piano.

My best Junior Church buddy was Bill

Bruhn. We always sat together and managed to stay out of trouble most of the time. One Sunday, Bill had a Vick's inhaler (remember those?) that he kept trying to stick up my nose for some odd reason. Even though I said the thing stunk, Bill thought it was funny to keep trying to make me smell it again. Mr. Eaton finally had to take it away from Bill because he was disrupting the service. I was glad because the inhaler smelled really strong and I didn't want it stuck in my nose after it had been in Bill's. Friendship had its limits.

After we sang several songs each Sunday morning, Mr. Eaton would tell us a Bible story, explain its meaning, and attempt to apply it in some way to our young lives. Sometimes, the applications made sense, sometimes they didn't. But the exposure to God's Word had some value whether we always understood it or not. We developed a respect for the Bible and what it said.

After Bible story time, there was a brief communion service. Most of us were still unbaptized and non-participants, but we always sat there and watched in awe as the adults and one or two of the older kids among us who were baptized partook of the broken soda crackers and little glasses of grape juice. We may not have fully grasped the concept of the body and blood of Christ at our age, but we learned to be quiet and respectful during this special time of remembrance. Next, we'd pass around an offering plate into which we deposited an assortment of loose coins. These and other funds were sent to help our missionaries (like Mrs. Gertrude Shoemaker in the Belgian Congo) take the good news to less fortunate people in Africa and other faraway places around the world.

At the conclusion of the Junior Church service, our assembly would break up into individual age groups. Each age went to its own classroom off the main meeting area. My favorite teacher was Charlie Anderson. By an odd coincidence, he was Bill Bruhn's brother-in-law, having married Bill's much-older sister. Mr. Anderson didn't cut Bill any slack, however, and made him mind the same as the rest of us.

The Sunday School lessons were most always interesting. Mr. Anderson often used unusual objects which he brought in a paper bag to illustrate the points he was trying to get across. I looked forward to sitting around the long table with the other kids, listening to his lessons, and wondering what would be in the bag that day. We'd often ask Mr. Anderson questions about the lesson—or any other subject on our young minds—and he'd try his best to answer them for us in a way that made sense. He was very patient and understanding; you could tell he really liked kids.

After graduating from Junior Church when I turned twelve, I began sitting with my parents during the morning worship services in the sanctuary. Reaching this milestone in my spiritual development made me feel like I'd really accomplished something. Our minister, Reverend Benton B. Miller, was stern-faced and always wore an old-fashioned black suit with striped pants and long tails on the coat. He had dark bushy hair and eyebrows and reminded me of a judge. His sermons, since they were primarily aimed at adults, were deeper in content than the sermonettes Mr. Eaton had presented in Junior Church. But enough of what Brother Miller preached soaked into me that I began realizing I was ready to become a follower of Jesus.

One Sunday morning while the invitation hymn was being sung, I slipped out of the pew and made the long walk down the aisle to the front of the sanctuary. Reverend Miller saw me coming and smiled (a rare occurrence). After the song ended, he took my confession of faith: "I believe that Jesus is the Christ, the Son of the living God and I accept him as my Lord and Savior." Then, he led me through one of the doors on the platform through which the choir entered and exited the sanctuary.

Another man met me there and showed me to a dressing room. He instructed me to remove my clothing and put on the white garments that he had laid out for me. The man said he would wait for me out in the hallway. I felt really strange taking my clothes off in church, but did as directed. The baptismal clothes were made of stiff, heavy linen. There was a pair of baggy pants that tied at the waist. They were kind of big on my skinny frame and I tied a good tight knot so they wouldn't fall down while I was walking to the baptistry. The short-sleeved upper garment didn't tie, it just had a large neck opening that slipped easily over my head.

When I was ready, the man led me to the stairway going down into the baptistry. Reverend Miller had just entered and was standing there in rubber waders with a white robe over them. I slowly went down the stairs into the unheated water. It felt really cold and I was half afraid my teeth would start chattering. I stood in front of Reverend Miller with his left hand resting lightly on my chest and his right hand raised over his head. I sneaked a quick look out of the corner of my eye at the congregation. I felt like everyone was looking directly at me. I was glad I didn't have to say anything because I was on the verge of getting the shakes.

Then in his deep voice, Brother Miller intoned some words about my confession of faith in Jesus and that he was now baptizing me in the name of the Father, the Son, and the Holy Ghost, for the forgiveness of my sins. I hadn't really committed too many transgressions that I was aware of at the tender age of twelve, but I was no angel. I wanted to have a clean slate in the eyes of God. So, I knew I was doing the right thing.

As soon as Reverend Miller finished his statement, his right hand came down to support the nape of my neck. With his other hand he pinched my nostrils shut and covered my mouth. Luckily, I remembered to gulp a breath of air just before he did this. Then, with a quick but gentle motion, he lowered me backwards into the water until I was completely submerged. I can still remember the surging sound the water made as it covered my ears. My immersion only took a second or two and I was back up on my feet, Reverend Miller patted me on the back and said, "God bless you."

After coming out of the water I may have looked the same as when I went in—except that now I was soaking wet from head to toe—but I was now one of the "saved." I'd been redeemed by the blood of Jesus Christ when he died on the cross. The congregation was singing "Now I Belong to Jesus" while I carefully climbed the slippery steps out of the baptistry and made my way back to the dressing room dripping a trail of water as I went.

After hurriedly drying off the best I could and getting dressed, I went back out into the sanctuary. The service had ended by then and several people were standing around waiting to congratulate me on making my big decision. Everyone was happy: me, my parents, my friends, Reverend Miller, and especially Mr. and Mrs. Eaton. They both gave me a big hug and told me how proud they were of me and what I'd done.

Who knows? Without the Eaton's love for and patient, caring work with young people, I might never have made that most important decision in my life. Someday, when I get to heaven, I plan to look them up and thank them both for setting my feet on the pathway to salvation. And my spiritual journey began in a red brick building housing a congregation of loving people called the Olive Branch Christian Church.

Eight years later, I married my high school sweetheart at Olive Branch. Four months after our marriage (while she was pregnant with the first of our four children) my wife, Joyce, made the same confession of faith that I had and was baptized in the same baptistry I was. The church building still stands today and looks exactly as it did when I went there as a boy.

Olive Branch Christian Church (Disciples of Christ) as it appears today—exactly the same as it did when I was attending there during the 1940s and '50s.

13

At the Movies

Three decades before I was born, there were nearly a dozen movie theaters in and around the Fountain Square area. As a result, this became known as the city's theater district during that period. By the time I was born in 1939, however, the number had dwindled to only three: the Fountain Square, on the east side of Shelby Street just south of Prospect; the Granada, on the south side of Virginia Avenue just north of Prospect; and the infamous Sanders, on the north side of Prospect, just east of Shelby.

My family often went to movies at the Fountain Square and Granada, but we never once attended the Sanders. It was the smallest of the three and had a bad reputation. When I became old enough to go to the movies with a buddy and without my parents, my folks absolutely forbade my going there. I think their prohibition had something to do with the fact that the Sanders was right next door to a tavern that sat on the northeast corner of Shelby and Prospect. It was no doubt a case of guilt by association, but they had the unshakeable notion that many patrons of the Sanders were public drunkards and other such lowlifes. I also remember hearing about some pervert being arrested in there after exposing himself to a boy in the restroom. This horror tale—whether true or not—did nothing to enhance the reputation of the Sanders in the eyes of my parents. In any case, it resulted in my never daring to set foot inside the place. In fact, the unsavory aura of the Sanders was so pervasive that I don't think I ever crossed over to the north side of Prospect in that block until I was an adult and needed to go to the hardware store located a couple of doors east of the theater.

The Fountain Square Theatre (they tried to project a high-class image by using the alternate spelling of theater) was the largest and my family's favorite. Part of its popularity was no doubt the fact that it was one of the first commercial buildings in the area to have air-conditioning. The large multistory building housing the Fountain Square Theatre also had a Hook's Drugstore on the corner and, of all things, a combination bowling alley and pool room upstairs on the fourth floor. On summer nights when the windows were open, you could hear the racket from the six lanes clear down on the sidewalk. Since I had no real interest in bowling as a kid, I never went up there myself—not even out of curiosity. It amazed me, however, how people in the various business offices could work in the same building with bowling balls thumping and pins crashing. Maybe the bowling alley didn't open until after the regular workday was over, so it wouldn't be a problem. Anyway, thanks to excellent sound-proofing, you couldn't notice any noise from the bowling alley when you were inside the theater.

The other "decent" theater in Fountain Square was the Granada. My family didn't attend there as often as we did the Fountain Square. The only outstanding memory I have of the Granada is the big red-and-white rubber floor mats in the outer lobby. The mats were always sticky when you walked across them—especially after they'd just been mopped. If people in those days had worn flip-flops (which hadn't been introduced to the world yet) , they likely would have lost them to the dreaded stickiness.

One thing that the Fountain Square and Granada theaters had in common was ushers. These were usually killjoys with big flashlights who would make kids be quiet if they got too noisy, or tell couples "making out" to please go upstairs to the balcony. I guess that's why the balcony became known as The Passion Pit. The ushers would also help you find seats if you arrived after the start of the movie. But their main purpose seemed to be maintaining a "family atmosphere" in the theater. While I was a teenager, I noticed that the ushers eventually went the way of floorwalkers in the downtown department stores. In other words, they disappeared forever. I guess they'd outlived their usefulness. More likely the declining number of movie-goers after the introduction of television meant that the theaters could no longer afford to keep the ushers working.

One other movie theater I remember attending a few times as a boy was the Oriental. This wasn't in Fountain Square, but was a small neighborhood theater on the east side of South Meridian Street about a block or so north of Morris. There were also a couple of other small south side movie theaters. One was the Lincoln (known to local kids fondly as "the stinkin' Lincoln" or "the Dink") on the east side of South East Street just north of Lincoln; the other was the Garfield on the east side of Shelby Street just south of Raymond. Both had their groups of loyal customers, but I was not one of them and never went to movies in either place. I almost forgot to mention one other small movie theater: the Avalon. It was on the south side of Prospect a few blocks east of Fountain Square. I have only a vague memory of being there once or twice.

Downtown Indianapolis had a multitude of movie theaters. I never attended any of these until after I became a teenager and got out on my own during my dating years while in high school. These theaters included the Circle, the

Indiana, Keith's, Loew's, the Lyric, the Ohio, and one called the Rodeo which—as you might guess—showed nothing but westerns. Since I was not a big fan of cowboy movies, I never went there or to the Ohio (which tended to show films a little too "adult" for teenagers). One other theater I never attended was the Walker. It was located a few blocks out Indiana Avenue on the northwest side of town in the black area.

If you grew up in the late 1940s and '50s like I did, you went to the movies almost every week—and maybe occasionally twice a week during the summer when school was out. Movie theaters used to show a new set of movies twice weekly. One double feature (that's *two* full-length movies) would play Monday, Tuesday, Wednesday, and Thursday. Another set of two would show Friday, Saturday, and Sunday.

One of the two movies shown would be an "A" picture, meaning that it featured the more popular movie stars, with better productions, and bigger budgets. Two "A" films were *never* shown on the same bill. Along with the featured movie would always be a "B" picture, most often a western, but sometimes a cops-and-robbers "crime doesn't pay" movie. These low-budget hack films were churned out by the hundreds. Even though I didn't care much for westerns or crime stories, I'd always sit through them to get my money's worth.

In those days, most movies were still

filmed in black-and-white. If a film was in color, it was an extra-special treat. Technicolor films were the best because they were in true-to-life colors. A cheaper alternative was called Cinecolor. Everything in these movies—mostly produced by Republic Pictures—appeared in predominant shades of brown, blue, and orange. Kind of weird-looking, but better than plain old black-and-white. Other movie innovations came along during my teen years when movies began having to compete with television. These included Cinemascope and VistaVision which required extra wide screens and bigger and better sound systems. The Fountain Square upgraded to show these movies; the Granada didn't. And the Sanders along with all the other neighborhood movie houses couldn't; they were far too small.

Another movie enhancement was called Cinerama. The Indiana was the only theater in Indianapolis—and maybe in the entire state—equipped to show such films. I went a couple of times as a teen and remember that the unusual projection booth sat down on floor level among the seats and used not one, but *three* projectors to fill the giant wraparound screen. Occasionally, you could notice the "seam" where two of the cameras were not running exactly in alignment. Cinerama movies usually played for several months at a time because they were much more expensive to produce. They turned out to be an interesting experiment, but they died out after a few years.

Yet another innovative attempt to improve movies was the 3-D (three-dimensional) process. This added realistic depth to the movie, but required special twin projectors showing overlapping images. Disposable glasses with polarized lenses were worn to produce the effect. The 3-D process really worked and I thought it was pretty wild to see things appear to fly off the screen and out into the audience so realistically that people would actually duck their heads and scream. The first 3-D movie was *The House of Wax* starring Vincent Price as the villain. The second such movie was a western with plenty of Indian arrows flying out of the screen. For some reason, 3-D movies didn't catch on in my day, although attempts have been made to revive them from time to time throughout the years since (including in the past year or two).

Along with the usual double feature at the movies, there was always a bunch of previews of coming attractions. A newsreel featured the latest highlights in national and world news and often showed unusual people, places, and occurrences. These were produced by either Movietone News or Pathé News. A man with a distinctive voice named Lowell Thomas narrated a lot of them. In addition to these extras, there would sometimes be a short subject, usually meaning a comedy film starring Leon Erroll, The Three Stooges (always my favorites), or some other popular comedians of the day.

As if all this wasn't enough, there would occasionally be a Burton Holmes travelogue showing the movie-goers some exotic location in a little-known part of the world where people observed strange customs. And there was *always* a cartoon, sometimes two. "Looney Tunes and Merrie Melodies" featuring Bugs Bunny, Elmer Fudd, and Daffy Duck were special favorites, as were the various Walt Disney characters like Mickey, Pluto, Donald, and Goofy. Woody Woodpecker had lots of fans, along with Oswald the Rabbit and other less-violent critters. I always enjoyed Popeye the Sailor Man and his constant crazy battles to save Olive Oyl from the clutches of Bluto (later renamed Brutus for some unknown reason), his archenemy.

During the World War II years (1941-1945), the newsreels always showed the latest war news and how we were winning over the evil Nazis (Germans) and the Japs (Japanese), sometimes called Nips (Nipponese). There would usually be a trailer (a very short film) showing the need for continuing to work hard in war production plants, the importance of saving scrap metal, or of keeping your eyes and ears open for any suspicious activity that might be enemy spies or saboteurs. These films usually ended with a pitch for everyone to go out and buy more War Bonds to help pay for the tremendous cost of the war. Even children were encouraged to buy War Stamps at their school, which could eventually be exchanged for regular bonds. Many of the feature films produced during these years focused on exciting and supposedly realistic war stories and made you leave the theater wanting to "kick a Kraut" or "slap a Jap." Of course, that was the main purpose of such films, to keep America united and morale high on the home front.

One other occasional feature at the movies that evidently had been popular in past years, but was dying out when I was a kid, were the so-called audience singalongs. Popular old songs like "Take Me Out to the Ballgame," "My Darling Clementine," and "Camptown Races" were played over the speakers while a short film clip accompanied it showing a supposedly typical movie theater audience smiling happily as they sang along with great enthusiasm. To help the audience members participate, the words of each song were spelled out across the bottom of the screen and a big white dot would jump from word to word and syllable to syllable. This was known as "following the bouncing ball." I never much cared for Hollywood musical movies, let alone these corny audience participation films. Most of us in the younger generation thought they were really silly and usually wouldn't sing. Soon, the days of the bouncing ball and audience singing went the way that silent films and theater organs had before our time. All I can say is good riddance.

On Saturdays, the theaters ran serials, long drawn out stories that lasted for several weeks in a row. Each weekly episode ended with what was called a cliff-hanger. This was some perilous situation in which the good guys seemed sure to face a gruesome death at the hands of the evil villain and his henchmen. When the next chapter started, however, the good guys were always miraculously saved by some person or factor that wasn't even shown in the previous ending. The obvious purpose of the serials was to get you hooked on the story line so you'd come back the following Saturday and keep it up through the entire series. These kid favorites were usually based on western themes, science-fiction (like Buck Rogers, Flash Gordon, and their cohorts), or even superheroes (like Superman).

Some serials defied categorization and were just plain one-of-a-kind. I remember one in particular that took place in a jungle. In every episode the hero and/or heroine had to make their way through the dreaded Valley of the Apes which featured a hundred or more gorillas standing on cliffs throwing big rocks down on people. Their aim wasn't too accurate because they never hit the good guys; but they sure could conk out the bad guys. I still marvel at where they got so many gorilla suits for this sappy production. I guess it was supposed to be scary, but when they showed the apes, all the kids would just laugh at them and cheer them on when they knocked out a villain. Ah, those were the days.

As a young kid, I didn't like horror films and my parents never took me or my sisters to see them. Unfortunately, the week before such films played, the audience was exposed to previews of them. I can remember more than once closing my eyes and hunkering down in my seat during previews of these movies starring such frightening creatures as The Mummy, Dracula, Frankenstein, and the Wolfman. As I grew older, however, I became fascinated by these monsters and others such as The Creature from the Black Lagoon. Eventually, I got to the point as a young teenager where I'd go see every scary movie there was. Most of them were pretty hokey and not at all like the blood-and-guts films of today.

Back then, the movie producers left something to the imagination instead of showing every gruesome detail. The mind conjured up far more frightening things than could be shown on film. And the movie rating system hadn't been introduced yet, so every film was considered a "family film." The only limitations were those imposed by public morals and a sense of decency. Unfortunately, both these safeguards eventually fell by the wayside and an official ratings system had to be implemented in their place.

The 1950s were the golden age of science-fiction movies. Creatures from outer space, mutated monsters, and gigantic bugs dominated the sci-fi films. I saw them all: *The Attack of the Fifty-Foot Woman, Them* (giant ants), *Tarantula* (a giant spider), *The Deadly Mantis* (a giant preying mantis), *Attack of the Giant Leeches* (really disgusting), *The Spiderwoman, Invaders from Mars, The Thing* (a real hair-raiser), *War of the Worlds* (one of the best sci-fi movies ever made), and many others too numerous to mention. I couldn't get enough of them even though they were crude by today's standards.

The success of the original *King Kong* movie (one of my favorites featuring both a giant gorilla *and* realistic dinosaurs), led to a number of far less-successful imitators such as *Son of Kong, Return to Kong Island, Mighty Joe Young*, and a little-known film called *Ponga: The White Gorilla*. I had nightmares about giant apes chasing me all over the place for years. Luckily, I finally outgrew them and had no lasting damage to my psyche. Well, at least none that I know of.

After I turned twelve and was allowed to go to the movies by myself, it almost became a Friday night ritual. I'd often meet my best buddy, Dick Foster, at the Fountain Square. After the movies I'd walk part way home with him and the rest of the way by myself. Some of those scary movies we saw left me a little nervous about venturing home alone in the dark. I was half afraid a zombie, or a gorilla, or some giant creature would jump out and get me. I'm glad to report that none ever did.

There were two kinds of movie fans: the popcorn eaters and the non-popcorn eaters. I was never a fan of theater popcorn, but always looked forward to buying a big roll of Necco Wafers. These were about the diameter of a quarter and maybe a little thicker and came in a wide variety of flavors. I never liked the licorice-flavored ones. Once I flipped one off the end of my finger to get rid of it and sent it sailing off into the audience. That was about the extent of my naughtiness as a kid. Other candy favorites of mine were DOTS and Chuckles (especially the red ones). You could buy a Holloway chocolate taffy sucker and still be working on it when the show ended and the big red velvet curtains closed. And these candies only cost a nickel or a dime back then.

Whenever Dick and I went to the movies, we always made sure to sit under the balcony and not in front of it. Some of the really mean kids would sit up there and throw stuff down on the audience: popcorn, candy wrappers, and occasionally a squirt or two from a water pistol.

One night at the Fountain Square things really got out of hand and someone tossed a water balloon off the balcony. Mr. Miller, the manager, had the projectionist stop the movie and turn up the house lights. Then he came out on the stage and warned the audience—especially those kids up in the balcony—that if the throwing stuff didn't stop he was going to end the show, *not* return our money, and clear the theater—plus call the cops. That sure got everyone's attention and the pranks stopped immediately (at least for that night). Still, it was always safer under the balcony. I never sat in a theater balcony until I started dating as a teenager and had something in mind other than childish pranks (if you know what I mean, and I'm sure you do).

When television started making a noticeable impact on movie attendance in the mid-'50s, the theaters tried a few new tricks to bring back the former movie-goers. Some revived "Dish Night" and, as the name implies, gave away free dishes. This had been tried with some success in earlier years during the Great Depression, but somehow free dishes just didn't have the magical drawing power of watching a flickering image on a box while sitting in your own living room. Many theaters began holding drawings for door prizes and tried other such gimmicks, but nothing seemed to work.

As a sad result, this is when movies began getting trashier, meaner, more spectacular, and bloodier and gorier. It began a downward spiral that continues to this day. The old restraints of public morals and decency were gone. The movie industry always says that their movies only *reflect* public taste, but I think in reality they *create* and *shape* public taste. The movies will never be like they were back in the good old days at the Fountain Square and the Granada. Kids today simply don't know what they're missing.

One last thing I almost forgot to mention was the price of movie theater admission back then. Kids got in for a QUARTER and adults paid FIFTY CENTS. So, going to the movies once or twice a week in those days was quite a bargain. Quite a bargain, indeed. And the place to be on Friday nights or at the Saturday matinees—or both, if you could swing it—was definitely at the movies.

"Th-th-that's all, folks!"

The Fountain Square Theatre building still stands today, but is now a conference center. The Granada Theater closed its doors in 1951 and was purchased by the G. C. Murphy Co. to expand its existing five and dime store which thrived for a couple of decades and eventually fell on hard times. Today, the building houses a collection of small shops and a restaurant. The Sanders Theater closed many years ago and the building burned in the late '90s. The rebuilt building now houses a used bookstore. All the other small neighborhood theaters were closed decades ago.

14

Who the Heck was Ben-Hur and Why is His Name on My New Bicycle?

On the Christmas right before I turned twelve, I received the ultimate gift that every young boy desired more than any other: a new bicycle. Several brands of bikes were available to choose from in those days. These included Columbia, J. C. Higgins (sold by Sears & Roebuck), Huffy (yes, they were around back then), Monarch, Murray, Roadmaster, Shelby, Western Flyer (sold by Western Auto supply stores), and—the absolutely most-desired of all—Schwinn.

The Schwinn was considered the Cadillac of bicycles. That's why every boy wanted one. I don't know why, maybe it was their paint job, or perhaps it was just the mystique that surrounded the brand name. Part of a Schwinn's great desirability was a special feature called knee-action, a unique suspension system on the front wheel not available on any other bike. This patented system consisted of an impressive chrome-plated spring jutting about three inches out from the front of the fork and attached to two struts that ran down to each end of a pivoting bracket on which the front axle was mounted. The spring was designed to absorb the shaking that usually results from hitting bumps and holes while riding a bike. Some other bikes had simple struts from the top of the fork down to the front axle, but none of them had the distinctive Schwinn spring shock absorber.

I had asked for a bicycle for Christmas that year and was fairly certain I would be getting one. I don't remember my parents asking me what *brand* of bike I wanted. If they did ask, I'm sure I told them I wanted a Schwinn. We were a typical working-class family with an adequate, but limited, income. So, asking for an expensive bike like a Schwinn was really pushing my luck. But, I dared to ask anyway.

I do remember as Christmas drew nearer trying to wheedle the name of the bike I was going to receive out of my father. I pestered him to death about it until he finally gave in and told me—but in a most unusual way. He said, "Son, I won't tell you the name of the bike you're going to get, but if you pronounce it *backwards* it sounds like Renneb." I always liked to play guessing games, but was totally mystified at this puzzle presented by my dad. *Renneb? Renneb? Renneb?* I wondered over and over again. *What could it mean?*

I tried turning the mysterious word around in my mind and it came out as Benner. I'd never heard of a bike called a Benner, but I knew one thing for certain: there was no way Benner sounded anything like Schwinn. Maybe Dad was trying to prepare me in advance and let me down easy so I wouldn't be so disappointed when I didn't get a Schwinn for Christmas. If that was his goal, he failed. And my hope for a Schwinn remained alive.

Christmas morning finally came. As we all gathered in the living room, still in our pajamas and nightgowns, I was surprised not to see a bicycle maybe covered with a bed sheet standing over in the corner. My sisters and I opened all our gifts until there was only *one* box left. Dad dug it out from behind the base of the tree stand and handed it to me with a big smile. The present was about the size of a shoe box and felt heavy. Gee, maybe I wasn't getting a bike for Christmas after all. After unwrapping the box, I found a smaller box inside—along with a couple of big pieces of wood that had made the box so heavy. I hurriedly opened the second box and found a tiny box inside. After opening this one, I discovered a note that said:

YOU HAVE ONE MORE GIFT,
BUT, IT'S IN HIDING.
AFTER YOU FIND IT
YOU'LL SOON BE RIDING.

A grin spread across my face; then, the real fun began. I started looking through the house for my hidden gift which obviously was a bicycle. My sisters followed me around in my search. Since our house was fairly small, I had a pretty good idea where my mystery gift must be hidden. But, I went along with the game and looked through the entire house first before finally heading for the rumpus room. We didn't use this room during cold weather because when it was added onto the back of the house many years previously no heat duct was provided. The rumpus room door off the kitchen was kept closed all winter to help keep the heat from our coal furnace contained in the rest of the house.

The entire family followed me as I hurried through the kitchen and slowly opened the door into the rumpus room. The cold air in the room made it feel like a meat locker. I immediately looked behind the door. And there it was: a large, odd-shaped object covered with a sheet. *Hmmm. Wonder what that could be?*

You could almost hear the girls say "ooh" as Dad told me to remove the sheet and see what was under it—as if we all didn't already know. As I pulled the sheet back, I still harbored the hope that the bike underneath would somehow turn out to be a Schwinn. But the magic didn't happen; my hope was in vain. It *wasn't* a Schwinn. As I uncovered the front of the bike, it was immediately obvious that there was no knee-action spring-and-strut assembly on the front wheel. The bike's nameplate wasn't the distinctive white oval bearing the simple word SCHWINN in black capital letters. I tried not to let it show, but my face must have betrayed my huge feeling of disappointment.

As I completed uncovering the bicycle and stood there looking at it, I didn't know what to say. After several seconds went by, my father asked me, "What's the matter, Charles? You said you wanted a bike for Christmas. You don't seem very excited about getting one."

I whined, "I did want a bike, but I really wanted a Schwinn."

Dad replied, "Well, we couldn't afford one of those, but this bike is just as good as a Schwinn." I didn't believe his words of consolation. In my mind, NO bike could possibly be as good as a Schwinn.

I wondered just what brand of bike this non-Schwinn was as I bent over and looked more closely at the nameplate mounted on the front of the fork. The oval-shaped plate was silver and heavily embossed with what appeared to be a man in a chariot using a long whip to drive a team of four galloping horses. Above the chariot were the two words "Ben-Hur." I instantly reversed the name in my mind and realized that it would be pronounced "Renneb" (or, more accurately, Ruh-neb) backwards. Dad had been correct in the reversed-name guessing game he'd played with me before Christmas. But he and Mom were way off the mark from satisfying my desire for a bicycle of another name, one starting with the letter S. Dad said, "I know you wanted a Schwinn, but give this bike a chance. The man at the store said it's well-made and they're built right here in Indianapolis." Somehow, that didn't matter to me and his praises fell on deaf ears.

As Dad continued his comments, I began looking my bicycle over more closely. I had to admit that it did have a good paint job. If your nose was close enough, you could even smell the thick enamel. I'd wanted a *red* Schwinn with *white* pin-striping. My Ben-Hur was *maroon* with *cream*-colored accents. At least maroon was a shade of red, but I'd have to get used to the cream trim. At least, the Ben-Hur was fully equipped with a light on the front fender, a boxed-in frame containing a button-activated horn, and a luggage rack over the back fender. The wheels were chrome-plated. *Hmm. This bike's no Schwinn, but maybe it's not so bad after all,* I thought.

The weather that day was bitterly cold. A few snow flurries were blowing in the wind, so I wasn't in any hurry to take my new bicycle outside and ride it. Later in the afternoon, after the flurries stopped and the sun came out for awhile, Dad encouraged me to take my bike for a test ride. So, I bundled up good and carefully guided the bicycle through the living room door, across the sun porch, through the front door, across the front porch, down the three steps to the walk, and out to the curb. I then mounted up and began riding my Ben-Hur for the first time. Since it was so cold, my family stayed inside and watched from the sun porch. The porch wasn't heated, but at least they were out of the wind.

As I pushed away from the curb, I noticed immediately how responsive the Ben-Hur was compared to my beat-up old, used bike I'd dubbed "Black Beauty" (because of the color I'd painted it). My old bike only had 24-inch wheels; my new one had big 28-inchers. And those larger tires did seem to make my new bike go much faster. Dad told me later that he thought maybe the Ben-Hur's drive-sprocket had a few more teeth on it than most other bicycles. That greater ratio between the front and back gears also likely contributed to my bike's speediness.

After riding up and down the block a few times, I spotted my friend, Jimmy Crose, starting to ride what must have been a new bike in his block of Wright Street on the other side of Sanders. He saw me and waved; we rode toward each other. As he came closer it was obvious that he, too, had received a new bicycle for Christmas. His was some English brand I'd never heard of, one of those fancy imported models with narrow tires, a three-speed gear shifter mounted on the handlebars, an air pump that clipped onto the frame, and a tool bag that hung down from the back of the seat. And not only did it have chrome wheels, his bike had chrome fenders. It wasn't a Schwinn, but it was a really neat bike. That lucky dog! Kids back then used to call bicycles like his "racing" bikes, but in reality they were touring bikes. The gears were to help their riders climb hills, not win races.

We stood there straddling our new bikes while we looked over at each other's and commented about their various features. Jimmy agreed with me that he'd never heard of a Ben-Hur either. Then, he said, "Hey, wanna race?" I said, "Sure. I gotta see just how fast this thing can go." We decided to start our race in front of Jimmy's house on the southwest corner of Wright and Sanders. We quickly agreed that we'd race down Wright Street for two blocks. The first one to cross Parkway would win. No one was watching us. It was just two buddies out to beat each other in a typical boyhood competition.

We lined up side-by-side a few feet apart. Looking at each other and grinning with cold faces, we chanted in unison as we nodded our heads with each word: "Ready . . . set . . . GO!" Jimmy might have had some advantage with his gears and jumped into an immediate lead. I was slower at first, but once I got my Ben-Hur rolling I began picking up speed and catching up with him. By the time we reached the half-way point, we crossed Orange Street side by side. Our hot breath was gushing out like two steam engines in the cold air. In the second block, I began gaining steadily and shot across Parkway two or three bike-lengths ahead of him. I was impressed; so was Jimmy. He said, "Hey, that thing really *is* fast." I grinned the best I could despite my half-frozen cheeks and agreed. By then, we were both so cold that we each headed for home. On my way back up Wright Street, I thought to myself, *Maybe a Ben-Hur's not such a bad bike after all. It does have a good paint job, and it sure is fast.*

Arriving back at the house, I pulled the bike inside and parked it in the enclosed sun porch temporarily. My riding was over for the day. As I went inside and took off my coat, sock hat, and gloves, Dad asked me, "So, how do you like your new bike now that you've ridden it?" I had to admit that it was pretty fast. I told him how I just beat Jimmy Crose on his new racing bike with its shiftable gears. Dad smiled and said, "See, I told you it wasn't a bad bike and that it was really fast." He was right, of course. It *wasn't* a bad bike and it *was* fast. But I still wondered, *Who the heck was Ben-Hur and why is his name on my new bicycle?*

I learned later that Ben-Hur was a heroic chariot driver in the classic book with that title written by Lew Wallace, a retired Civil War general from the Union army. That explained the mysterious image on the nameplate of my new bicycle. My bike might as well have been custom-built just for me because I never saw another Ben-Hur during my entire boyhood. After finding out the origin of its name, and eventually discovering that I could beat *any* bike in my neighborhood—including Schwinns with their fancy knee-action suspension—I learned not only to like my bike, but to LOVE it. My Ben-Hur got me around for several years until I reached that awkward age: too old to be seen riding a bike, but still too young to drive a car.

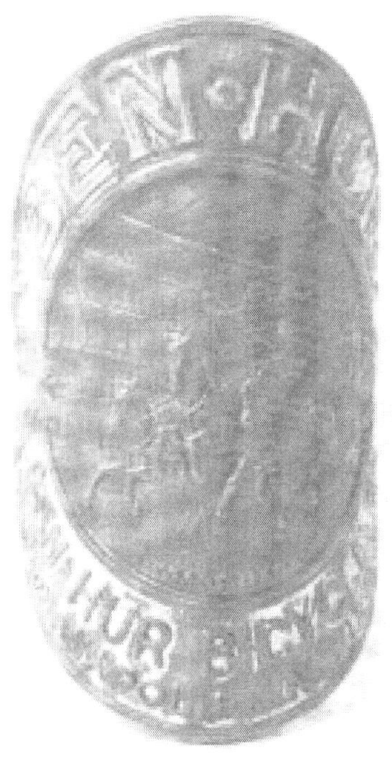

Logo nameplate from the fork of a Ben-Hur bicycle (enlarged about twice actual size to show details).

15

Losing My Marbles

One thing I knew for certain during the three years I had a paper route was that I'd be out collecting most every Saturday. On one such day, I was riding my bike down Sanders Street to catch a couple of my delinquent customers. I came upon a bunch of boys all kneeling down on the ground around something obviously of great interest. They were out in front of the Quinnette's house in the grass strip between the sidewalk and the curb. Only in this case it wasn't grass; it was a patch of bare dirt.

As I pulled up and stopped, I saw that the boys were gathered around a circle about two feet in diameter scratched in the dirt. Inside the circle was an assortment of marbles. I'd heard of kids playing marbles before, but had never actually seen anyone doing it. One of the boys I knew looked up and asked me the *first* fateful question, "Wanna play?"

I'd never played marbles in my life, but the guys sure looked like they were having a lot of fun. So, I replied, "Yeah. But I'll have to go get my marbles." I forgot all about collecting and quickly pedaled home. Even though I was a marble-shooting novice, I did have a small collection. They'd originally been my dad's when he was a boy. They were in a little cloth drawstring bag that his mother had made for him out of a scrap piece of material. I'd found the marbles on one of our visits to Granny White's house in Dad's little country crossroads hometown of Stilesville. The marbles, along with some other odds and ends from his boyhood, were in an old wooden crate in a corner of Granny's pump house. Dad had been surprised they were still around and seemed pleased that I wanted them. I'd kept them among my special treasures for a few years, but had never played with them.

I arrived back at the big marble game, got off my bike, and parked it nearby. In no time I was down on my knees with the rest of the guys. I reluctantly admitted my ignorance of how to play and my total lack of experience at doing so. One of the kids explained the rules and told me that all rounds were being played "for keeps." I watched the others play for a few minutes to see how it went. Shooting marbles didn't look too difficult; I thought I could do it.

Little did I know that my ignorant optimism would soon be shattered by the reality that it wasn't nearly as easy as it looked.

Finally, a new round was started and I was included. All I remember about the game is that I couldn't shoot marbles worth a hoot. Before I knew it, I'd lost ALL my marbles (about twenty-five) to Tommy, the youngest of the three Quinnette brothers, who was cleaning everyone's clock. He looked across the circle and asked me the *second* fateful question of the day: "Wanna play double-or-nuthin'?"

Again, I wasn't sure exactly how that worked, so he quickly explained that just he and I would play another round. If I won, I'd owe him nothing and he'd even give me back the marbles I'd already lost. On the other hand, if I blew this round I would owe him *double* the amount of marbles I'd already lost. It sounded like an easy way to recoup my losses, so I quickly agreed. What a mistake that turned out to be. Tommy generously loaned me some of the marbles he'd won from me so I could play in the double-or-nothing shoot off.

This kid must have been the uncrowned marble-shooting champion of the south side. He was just a little squirt. But, boy, could he shoot marbles. My skill didn't improve under pressure and my luck didn't either. I lost another round and owed him twenty-five more marbles for a total of fifty. Then, he asked me the *third* fateful question: "Wanna go again?" Why I didn't stop right there I'll never know. But I went another round, lost again, and owed him a *hundred* marbles total. Now, I was getting steamed. We went another round and another.

Same story. I lost both times. I finally threw in the towel and said, "That's enough. I quit." No boy ever wanted to be branded a quitter, but my losses drove me to it. I *had* to quit.

The other boys around the circle couldn't believe I'd lost 400 marbles. Some of them laughed while others just shook their heads not knowing what to say. Several of them made wisecracks about my defeat while all I could do was sit there and take it. I told Tommy he'd already won all the marbles I owned and I'd have to go buy more to pay him off. He said okay. I promised to bring them to him before the end of the day. I knew better than to try to welsh on him. He had two bigger brothers who I didn't want to tangle with, even though they were nice guys and probably wouldn't do anything to me.

I headed back home to get some money out of the old cigar box in the dresser drawer where I kept my cash stashed. I didn't even tell my mother I was going to Fountain Square or why. That would have led to some questions I didn't want to answer about my humiliating loss. She just thought I was going back out on my paper route to continue collecting. Yes, I'll admit I could be a little sneaky at times like this.

After arriving at the G. C. Murphy Five & Dime Store, I went to the toy and game counter. There I found exactly what I needed: small net bags containing twenty-five marbles each. Some were all solids; some were what I heard the kids call “swirlies.” I bought all fourteen bags they had out on display and asked the lady behind the counter if they had any more in stock. She checked and said no. Darn it! I was still twenty-five marbles short of what I owed Tommy. It would have to do; I didn’t know where else to buy marbles, at least not within the range I was allowed to ride my bike.

The clerk put the bags of marbles inside a doubled brown paper sack. Let me tell you, 350 marbles weighed what seemed like ten pounds—maybe more. I had to steer my bike using only my right hand, so that I could hold onto the sack of marbles with my left. I rested the sack on my upper leg to support it. Luckily, I made my way back to Tommy Quinnette’s without any mishap. As I pulled up in front of his house, I saw that the marble tournament was over and all the kids had disappeared. Tommy had probably cleaned them all out. I was really glad there were no witnesses around to see my embarrassing payoff.

I lugged the heavy sack up the stairs to the Quinnette’s front porch and knocked on their screen door by kicking the bottom with my foot. Here came Tommy, all smiles. He’d probably been counting the bucketful of marbles he’d won from everybody. I handed him the big sack and said, “Here ya go. I bought all the marbles Murphy’s had, but I’m still twenty-five short of what I owe ya.” Tommy had so many marbles he could afford to have mercy on me and said, "Aw, that's close enough. We'll call it even." I left with my funds seriously depleted, but with my honor still intact.

I climbed on my bike and went back to collecting along my paper route—something I should have kept doing in the first place instead of trying to play marbles with kids who really knew how. I'd just looked at it as a harmless game. Even though skill and luck were involved, shooting marbles "for keeps" was still kind of like gambling—especially the double-or-nothing part. And my parents had taught me that gambling was wrong. How right they were. How very right. As always.

I may have lost all my marbles that day, but I did learn a valuable lesson. As a result of this childhood experience, I never gambled again till late in my adult life. No tip boards, no penny ante poker, no participation in office pools, no bets, no trips to Las Vegas. I was well into my late fifties before I even dared to buy a lottery ticket now and then when the jackpots grew ridiculously large. I'd like to tell you that I was a big winner, but I never was. Whether it's playing for hundreds of marbles or mega-millions of dollars, I've always been a loser when it comes to gambling.

16

One Wild Afternoon

One sizzling summer afternoon my buddy, Jimmy Crose, and I were messing around on our bikes in the shade of some tall trees out behind his house. It was too hot to do much of anything, but Jimmy came up with a good idea. He said, "Let's go down to the Barnett's and see what they're up to." I knew Jimmy and the two Barnett brothers were pals, but I didn't really know them, even though they lived on my paper route. Since I had an hour or so to kill and nothing better to do, I said, "Sounds okay to me, let's go."

Jimmy led off and we pedaled slowly down Sanders Street. We turned in at a house where the front yard was mostly bare dirt with a few scattered clumps of uncut grass and weeds. We got off our bikes, walked them across the dusty yard, and parked them beside the front porch where two boys were sitting. After we all said "hi" to each other, Jimmy introduced me to the Barnetts. They were a little younger than me and didn't look much like brothers. Wiley Barnett was a tad bigger and maybe a year older than his kid brother, Darrell. Wiley had tanned skin and brown hair; Darrell was fairer skinned and had lighter hair. They both grinned in a friendly way and turned out to be the kind of guys you couldn't help but like right off the bat.

They told us their dad was at work and their mom was gone for a couple of hours, so they were home by themselves. Since it was one of those hot-enough-to-fry-an-egg-on-the-sidewalk kind of days, the boys said to come on in and we'd find something cold to drink. We all filed inside and headed for their kitchen.

Wiley told us they didn't have any soda pop, but their mom had fixed them a pitcher of Kool-Aid before she left. We could have that or we could have ice water. Naturally, we all chose the Kool-Aid. It's bright red color was definitely more appealing than plain old water. Darrell cracked open a tray of ice cubes from their fridge and plopped several into four glasses. Then, Wiley filled them up nearly brimful. We sat there around their kitchen table like real men of the world drinking cherry Kool-Aid from our tall, dripping glasses. Since there was no air conditioning in those days, it was so hot inside their house that our sweaty arms kept sticking to the tabletop. We laughed about it as we brushed stray crumbs off our arms.

As boys will often do, we got to talking about typical boy stuff. After we spent several minutes sharing some stories and jokes and maybe telling a kidding lie or two, Wiley asked Jimmy and me an unexpected question that grabbed our attention. "Have you guys ever seen a picture of a naked woman?" Suddenly, there was dead silence while Jimmy and I looked at each other in surprise. We reluctantly admitted that neither of us had. Wiley grinned real wide and said, "Do ya wanna see one?" Well, as you can imagine, we both did. What boy could turn down an offer like that?

Wiley left the three of us sitting there for a minute and soon returned with a slightly curled, black-and-white photo of a smiling woman. She was lying on her back in the middle of a double bed. Wiley hadn't been kidding; she was buck naked alright. Oh, was she ever. My mouth hung open in amazement while my virgin eyes crawled over her shapely body taking in every detail. The triangular patch at the top of her thighs was as black as the long, wavy hair on her head and the large, round dark spot on each boob stood out like a bull's-eye on a target. My mind wrestled with opposing feelings. Somehow, I knew that I shouldn't be looking at such a picture, yet at the same time I really wanted to. "Really-wanted-to" quickly won out, so I kept soaking it all in.

"Wow!" I exclaimed. "Where'd you get this?" It looked like a regular snapshot you might see in a family photo album, except for the way-out-of-the-ordinary subject matter.

Wiley looked over at Darrell and they both snickered.

Then, Wiley said, "We found it in a dresser drawer in our folks' bedroom."

Darrell chimed in, "That's our mom." He sounded almost proud when he said it.

"She is not," I said. I thought he was pulling my leg.

"Cross my heart and hope to die," he replied.

Wiley backed up his brother's claim and said, "No kiddin', that really is *his* mom. She's my stepmom." He followed that up with one more question, "So, whadayya think?" and gave us another sly grin.

I nearly choked on the ice cube in my mouth and took one more long look. What do you say in a situation like that? I didn't know whether to make any further comments or not, so simply said, "Well, guys, . . . uh, . . . she sure is pretty." I knew my face must have turned several shades redder than it already was from being so hot because the Barnetts both laughed when I said it.

Jimmy looked at the picture next, but not for nearly as long as I had. He didn't say much either, except to agree with my somewhat evasive answer. That was the only such photo the boys had to show us and Wiley hurried to put it back where it belonged before his mother came home. While he was gone, I sat there crunching the remains of an ice cube and thought about what had just happened. I didn't say anything about it, but I couldn't understand how these guys could look at a photo of their own mother (or stepmother) naked, let alone show it around to other boys—even though I was one of those boys and really hadn't minded seeing it.

After that bit of excitement died down and we were nearing the bottom of our glasses, the Barnetts started talking about another favorite subject of every boy: guns. They bragged that they each owned a BB rifle. Neither Jimmy nor I had one. Wiley and Darrell asked us if we wanted to see theirs. We sure did. So, they went to their bedroom and each returned proudly carrying a Daisy air rifle. I don't know about Jimmy, but my parents (especially my overly protective mother) would *never* allow me to have a BB gun. She thought they were far too dangerous. After all, they could shoot someone's eye out. Every parent knew that, especially *my* parents. As a result, I had absolutely no hope of ever owning a BB gun. I knew better than to ask for one for Christmas and I was certain that my folks wouldn't even have let me buy one with my own money.

We looked the rifles over carefully and admired them while the Barnetts showed us how they worked. The boys were willing to let us shoot their rifles if we wanted to. And, of course, we did want to. So, we all went out into their backyard and fired quite a few shots at some tin cans we dug out of the trash. I soon discovered that shooting cans was a whole lot of fun, especially when you heard that satisfying "donk" sound and saw your target fall over. I don't know what my mom was so worried about; shooting BB guns seemed perfectly harmless to me.

After twenty minutes or so passed and the novelty of target shooting out in the broiling sun wore off a bit, Wiley had a better idea. "Hey, how about having a *real* gun battle?" Jimmy and I were all-too-easily convinced by the enthusiastic Barnetts that this would be even more fun than plinking at tin cans. In the back of my mind, however, a little voice tried to tell me that maybe this *wasn't* such a great idea. I'd seen what a BB could do when it hit a metal can; what might one do that hit any of us? But I kept quiet about my concern and went along with the other guys.

Wiley and Darrell talked like they'd had shootouts several times before and they began telling us how we'd do it. Darrell and Jimmy would be out in the Barnett's garage at the back of their property while Wiley and I'd be in the house. Each team would share a gun and take turns shooting at the other two guys. Again, that nagging little voice: *Sounds like fun, but it sure seems like someone could get hurt doing this*. In the excitement of the moment, the voice quickly faded away.

We hurried to take up our positions. Darrell and Jimmy headed for the garage. They opened a hinged window and swung it back out of their way so they could shoot toward the house through the opening. Wiley and I returned to the kitchen where the window was already wide open. He said we needed to take out the screen so the other guys wouldn't shoot any holes in it (it looked like it'd already been punctured a few times during their previous battles). I thought how strange it was to worry about that when no one seemed the least concerned about shooting holes in one other. Anyway, we unhooked the wooden frame and pushed the screen out so it fell flat on the ground. We then had a clear field of fire toward the garage (a distance of maybe twenty-five or thirty feet).

The gun battle started right away. The air rifles had to be pumped up with a built-in hand lever before each shot. Wiley gave ours an extra pump or two to make sure it fired at maximum power. Then, he handed me the gun. I carefully took aim and fired my first shot. I heard it hit the side of the garage, but I don't think it was any ways near the window. After alternating several turns, it became obvious that the Barnetts were much better shots than Jimmy and me.

We all exchanged fire for several minutes.

Our goal wasn't really to shoot the other guys, just to put our shots through their window and scare them. Sometimes, I'd see or hear a BB come through the kitchen window, ricochet off the wall behind us, and bounce onto the linoleum floor. I have to admit, it was pretty exciting—just like in the movies when cowboys, or cops and robbers, or soldiers were in blazing gun battles.

The next time it was my turn, I cautiously peeked up over the window sill, and—ZING!—a BB grazed my left cheek just below my eye. I yelped, "Oww!" and ducked my head. My wound wasn't bad, but it stung a little—okay, it stung a lot. When I dabbed at it with my hankie, I saw there was hardly any blood. I lucked out and only got a scratch.

Wiley hollered for the other guys to stop shooting because I'd been hit. Jimmy and Darrell came running to see how badly I was shot. Even though it was just a little scratch, they made over it like it was really something. I felt like a battle-scarred hero. My injury must have scared Wiley enough that he decided—and we all wisely agreed—that maybe we should end the battle before anyone else got hurt. Besides that, their mother might return early and catch us right in the middle of our shootout. I think that was more likely the real reason for our sudden cease-fire. By then it was also about time for me to go pick up my newspapers and deliver them on my afternoon route.

Jimmy and I thanked the Barnett boys for letting us shoot their air rifles and told them how much fun we'd had. Darrell said he was sorry I got shot, likely because he fired the BB that nicked me. But I didn't hold it against him; it was just an accident. We all said our "see-ya's" and Jimmy and I took off on our bikes.

We rode together back to Jimmy's where I headed on around the corner and up Wright Street for home. I went inside very quietly and picked up my saddle-bags. Mom was busy in the kitchen and I carefully avoided her so she wouldn't get a chance to see my battle scar. After I was back outside, I yelled in through the kitchen screen door that I was leaving to go get my papers. She said okay and didn't see my face to notice the wound.

Unfortunately, Mom did notice the scratch on my cheek during supper and asked me about it. (I knew she would and I was dreading it.) I may have acted like a stupid kid now and then, but at least I was an honest kid—well, mostly honest, most of the time. I confessed and told her about being over at the Barnett boys' house and how they had BB guns and were shooting at some targets and that somehow I'd gotten zinged (I didn't want to use a scary word like "shot" or "hit"). What I told her was the truth, it just wasn't the whole truth.

I didn't mention the fact that I'd participated in a gun battle and implied that I was only a bystander while someone else shot the stray BB that grazed me. Mom was *not* pleased to learn about my reckless behavior in being around other boys while they were shooting guns. I could tell she was really upset. And I mean really.

"See," she said while shaking her finger at me across the table to emphasize her words. "That's the very reason why I don't want you to *ever* have a BB gun, Charles Edward." (She only called me by my full name when I was in serious trouble.) Dad nodded his silent agreement with a somber look on his face. I imagined that he was already deciding how many licks with the razor strap I deserved for my foolhardiness. My two sisters just sat there wide-eyed while I took the heat. "You could have been shot in the eye and blinded for the rest of your life, young man. Did you even stop to think about that?" Her accusing finger finally stopped wagging, but her eyes were still glaring. I didn't know what to say. "Well, did you?" she added impatiently.

I started to tell her that actually I had thought about it—but it hadn't stopped me. So, I didn't even bother to mention it. After a few more awkward moments of silence staring down at my plate, I looked up and said meekly, "No, ma'am. I'm sorry. I guess I didn't." She was right and I knew it. And, more importantly, she knew that I knew it. As a result of her strong words (and because I was hoping to avoid punishment), I voluntarily promised Mom and Dad that I'd never go over to the Barnett's house again. And I kept my promise. But I'll always remember that day when I first tasted the double forbidden pleasures of naked women and blazing guns. It was one wild afternoon.

17

A Trip to the Shoe Store and Challenging the Wall of Death

Twice a year (in time for Easter and again before the fall school semester started) Mom took my two sisters and me shopping for new shoes. There were three shoe stores in Fountain Square back when we were kids: Merit's, Schiff's, and Thomann's. Our mother was a loyal Thomann's customer; we never even set foot inside the other two shoe stores. Thomann's was located on the southwest corner of Prospect and Shelby. An older German gentleman and his middle-aged son owned and operated the store, and had for many years. The senior Mr. Thomann reminded me of the actor who played The Wizard of Oz. He was short and stocky, wore silver-framed glasses, had a square jaw, and sported a full, gray moustache to match his gray hair. I'm pretty sure he wore a toupee, although my mother sternly warned me never to mention it while in his store.

Mr. Thomann always seemed jovial whenever we saw him—probably because he knew he was guaranteed to sell three pairs of shoes whenever the White kids trooped in. The junior Mr. Thomann was quite a bit taller than his father, slender, mostly bald, and also wore glasses, but no toupee. He was always friendly, but wasn't as happy-natured as his father. Our mother preferred dealing with the elder Mr. Thomann for some reason. If he was busy with another customer, she'd wait patiently for him, while we kids sat there and squirmed not-so-patiently.

Thomann's Shoe Store was long and narrow and had a very high ceiling covered with embossed metal panels. Both the longer side walls were lined floor-to-ceiling with wooden shelves loaded with boxes of shoes. A wooden ledge twelve-inches or so wide ran along both walls of shelves, about two feet above the floor. The shelves below the ledge extended out further than the ones above it. Old Mr. Thomann (even at his age) would climb up on the ledge to reach shoes on the upper shelves when necessary. He sometimes used a long pole with a specially shaped hook on the end for pulling down boxes that were way up near the ceiling.

The store was brightly lit by white glass globe fixtures hanging down from long chains, similar to the lights in older schools. The floor was carpeted from wall to wall so that when you walked back and forth while trying on a pair of shoes you wouldn't mar the soles. And, as you would expect, a double row of chairs ran from the front to the back of the store.

Thomann's had a most unusual device that never failed to fascinate my sisters and me whenever we were there. A mysterious wooden cabinet about four feet tall with a short platform on the front housed an in-store X-ray machine. When you stepped up on the platform and stuck your feet inside a slot in the cabinet's base, the machine came on and began making a low humming sound. Then, we, Mom, and Mr. Thomann, could look down through an oval-shaped viewing port on top of the cabinet and see a strange, greenish glow revealing ghostly images of the bones inside our feet and toes, as well as the outline of the shoes we were trying on.

This machine showed how well the shoes fit, or didn't fit. I think our mother was impressed by this technology and that's one reason she always brought us to Thomann's for our shoes. We kids thought it was really neat to actually see our bones. I'd sometimes slip over and stand in the machine when Mom and Mr. Thomann were busy finding shoes for one of my sisters. I'd wiggle my toes and watch them move. My sister Sandy usually followed my bad example when I felt generous enough to allow her to have an extra turn in the bone box. Mr. Thomann was pretty smart to offer such incentives that kept his customers coming back. Heaven knows what harmful dosages of radiation we received in those days before these devices were finally removed from shoe stores because of health concerns.

After Mom paid for our shoes, Mr. Thomann would wrap each box with heavy green paper and tie the bundle with dark green string. The paper was on a big roll in a holder at the end of the counter. A weighted metal bar with a sharp edge rubbed against the roll and was used for tearing off pieces to the desired length. The string was on a tall conical spool that spun on a spindle mounted atop the paper roll holder. We usually saved the string when we got home and kept it for other uses in the future. I'm not sure what my sisters did with their empty shoe boxes, but I always kept mine. They were useful for storing my growing collection of the kinds of stuff that boys liked to save back then. This included things like silver pennies, four-leaf clovers, buckeyes, unusual-shaped rocks, marbles, and other odds and ends that I found and treasured.

After wrapping our new shoes, Mr. Thomann would pull a box of trinkets out from under the wrapping counter and let us each pick one. These were small prizes similar to the ones found in boxes of Cracker Jack back then. But we thought they were really something. Naturally, this made us want to return to Thomann's the next time we needed shoes. What a treat! Playing in the X-ray machine *and* prizes too. Mr. Thomann was a pretty smart old bird to offer such incentives to keep his customers coming back.

While Mom was paying for our shoes, I'd usually walk over by the open top of a Dutch door nearby and watch the shoe repairman busily at work. His repair area was in the back corner of Thomann's, beside the rear entrance on Prospect Street. The repair shop had a very distinct odor that was a combination of leather, rubber, glue, and shoe polish. I liked that smell and can still remember it today. The cobbler was often too busy to notice me as I stood there watching him work away. But, sometimes, he might look up for a moment and give me a nod and a brief smile.

In those days, people took better care of their shoes and often had them resoled and reheeled instead of buying new ones. I can still remember seeing the repairman take a big handful of tacks and put them into his mouth like he was *eating* them. Then, he'd take the tacks out one at a time from between his lips with the magnetized head of his hammer. With a quick stroke, he'd bang each tack precisely into place around the edge of the soles on the shoes or boots he was repairing. He never missed.

Putting tacks in his mouth sure looked dangerous and I was curious if he ever swallowed any of them. One time when we were there, I got up my nerve and asked him. He chuckled and said, "Yes, young fella, I've swallowed a few in my day—but I try real hard *not* to." I couldn't imagine what it must feel like to swallow a tack. "Does it hurt when you swallow them?" I asked. He just smiled and said, "They don't hurt much going down, it's when they come out that you have to worry about." He gave me a sly wink and returned to his work.

Old Mr. Thomann was a nice man, but I had one gripe against him. When I was around twelve years old, I really, really wanted a pair of penny loafers which were in style at the time. My mother didn't think I should wear loafers because they wouldn't give my feet proper support while they were still growing. And wouldn't you know, Mr. Thomann, who Mom considered a shoe expert, fully agreed with her. As a result, I *never* got my penny loafers. I was suspicious that the *real* reason Mr. Thomann was against the loafers was that he didn't have any in stock and didn't want to lose a sale. This was just one of several childhood disappointments I suffered. But I soon got over it. And, who knows? Maybe Mr. Thomann was right and I was better off not wearing shoes that didn't provide proper support. In any case, I still ended up a few years later having flat feet. At least my mother had the satisfaction of knowing they didn't get that way because I wore penny loafers.

The elder Mr. Thomann lived on Leonard

Street where it made a jog at Orange Street. His house sat up on the side of a hill and a tall, concrete retaining wall ran along the south side of his property at the top of the T intersection where the hillside had been cut away to put the street through. The wall was at least eight feet high—maybe ten, possibly even *twelve* feet. I'd say the wall was about eight inches wide and maybe sixty or seventy feet long. It was *huge*. Most boys in the neighborhood at some time or other had walked along the top of Thomann's wall to prove their bravery—or their foolhardiness, depending on how you looked at it. Only a dumb kid would be crazy enough to try such a stunt. If you lost your balance, the fall to the sidewalk that ran beside the wall would likely have killed you, or surely would have resulted in crippling injuries.

So, being the dumb kid that I sometimes was, I started across the top of the wall one day on my way home from school just to see if I could do it. No one was around to watch or applaud my daring feat—thank heaven. I was doing okay at first, as long as I kept looking at the top of the wall slightly ahead of my feet. But, after advancing a distance of three or four yards, I made the mistake of looking down at the sidewalk far below. I stopped and immediately began having second thoughts about the wisdom of my venture.

Common sense prevailed. I ever-so-carefully turned around, went back to where I'd started, and climbed down off the wall without any mishap. As I did, I happened to look up and see Mrs. Thomann watching me out her window with a stern look on her face and shaking her head back and forth. I took off running and ran most of the remaining way home so she wouldn't come out and catch me as I passed by the front of her house. Luckily, she didn't know who I was or she might have called my mother and I would have had a warm reception waiting for me when I arrived home a few minutes later.

That was the one and only time I ever dared to challenge Thomann's infamous Wall of Death. And it's probably a good thing I never tried again. With my poor track record of near-fatal experiences while growing up, the odds were no doubt against me. But I'll always wonder if I *could* have made it. Without witnesses, no one would have believed me even if I had succeeded. So, maybe in this case, it's better to wonder than to know.

18

Crash Landing

Dick Foster was my best buddy since our days at School #13 when we were flag boys together in the fifth grade. As we got a little older and had bicycles, we often went riding around just for the heck of it. One summer afternoon Dick came by and wanted to know if I was up for a ride to his grandpa's house. I said I sure was, so off we went—*after* I got permission from my mom, of course.

Dick's grandpa was a wiry little Irishman with a good sense of humor. He lived on Regent Street, a block or so east of South Meridian down near Raymond Street. This was a couple of miles from my house, but that distance was no problem for two energetic kids like us riding bikes. We rode down South East Street, across Raymond, up Pennsylvania a block, and turned onto Regent. As we pulled up in front of Dick's grandpa's house, "Pop" (as Dick and everyone else called him) spotted us from his porch swing. He got up and started walking out to the curb. As he did, Dick took off on his bike and began riding back up Regent. He yelled, "Hey, Pop. Watch this." Then, after making a U-turn, Dick raced toward us at a speed obviously way too fast for the remaining distance. And I mean *way* too fast. I stood there astride my bike wondering what on earth he was up to.

At the last possible second, Dick reversed his pedals and activated his bike's coaster brake. As he did, we heard a loud CRACK! as his chain broke. This meant his bike instantly had *no* brakes. At this point it was too late to swerve and Dick plowed full speed into the rear bumper of his grandpa's car parked out in front of the house.

I couldn't believe what happened next; it was all so quick, yet seemed like it was in slow motion. As Dick's bike came to an instant stop, Dick didn't. He literally flew off the bike seat, up over the handlebars, and landed on his head on the trunk of his grandpa's car with an audible THUMP! As Dick lay there spread-eagle and momentarily stunned, what was Pop's reaction? He just bent over laughing, slapped his knee, and said, "That's a pretty good one, Richard. What other tricks can you do?" By then Dick had staggered to his feet and was holding his forehead. A big bump was already starting to form. Pop said, "Come on in here you dang fool. Let's put some ice on that goose-egg before it gets any bigger."

We went inside and Pop quickly grabbed some ice cubes out of the tray from his fridge and packed them into an old rubber ice bag.

Dick held the bag on his forehead for fifteen or twenty minutes while the three of us rehashed his trick and laughed about his unexpected flight and crash landing. After we finished drinking the glasses of ice water Pop gave us, Dick felt well enough to be concerned about his bike.

While Dick sat on the porch swing holding the ice bag on the top of his forehead, I went out and stood his bike up from where it was still lying behind Pop's car. The car was okay and wasn't even dented from Dick's impact—cars were built out of heavier gauge steel and had sturdier bumpers in those days. I wasn't surprised, however, to find that Dick's bike had suffered damage from the collision. The fork was bent back so far that the front fender hit against the frame and made steering impossible. I held the front tire off the ground and walked the bike up to the porch.

Pop came down and looked the bike over as I pointed out the problem. He said, "Aw, we can fix that." He shuffled around to the back of his house and out to his garage, returning in a few minutes with a small toolbox. After he dug out a couple of wrenches, we took off the front tire. Then, with the ends of the fork resting on the sidewalk and Dick and I pressing down with all our combined weight on the handlebars, Pop slowly pulled upward on the frame. He wasn't a big man, but was strong for his size. After several tries, little by little, the fork was bent forward near enough to its original position that the fender once again cleared the frame—but the clearance was mighty thin.

We patched a couple of splits in the inner tube from the front tire of Dick's bike and reassembled it inside the casing. Pop found an air pump out in his garage. It was rusty and squealed each time we pumped it, but it worked well enough to reinflate Dick's tire. After remounting the wheel, the bike still wasn't right, but it was rideable. The front rim was warped from the force of Dick's crash; it wobbled so badly that it barely cleared the insides of the fork. Dick's beat-up bike looked like one that a clown would ride in the circus. Somehow, that imagery seemed very appropriate.

Now, we had only one problem remaining: the broken chain. Unless it was repaired, Dick had no propulsion or brakes. After closer examination, we found that the chain had parted at the connecting link used to fasten the two ends into a continuous loop. The snap link was bent, but, again, Pop said we could fix it. He took a pair of heavy pliers and held the end of the link that was still attached to the chain. Then Dick grasped the other end of the bent link with another pair of pliers and applied pressure. Sure enough, after much grunting and straining, the link straightened out. After rethreading the chain around the front and rear sprockets,

Pop snapped the link into place. "Good as new," he declared with a grin and a chuckle. Well, maybe the chain was, even though the bike itself would never be the same.

Dick and I noticed the sky was rapidly clouding up and it was getting really dark out for that time of the afternoon. We quickly decided we'd better head for home. After thanking Pop for his help, Dick and I told him goodby and climbed on our bikes. As we pedaled off down Regent Street hoping to beat the rain that was obviously on its way any minute, Pop yelled at Dick, "Don't try any more of those damn fool stunts, Richard. You might break your neck next time." Dick hollered back over his shoulder, "Don't worry. I won't." But we all three knew good and well that he would.

Pop's name was Emmett McCray. He worked as a custodian at School #35 on East Raymond Street beside Madison Avenue for many years and was well-liked by all the kids and their teachers. Since the school was only a few blocks from his house, Pop walked to work. He trudged through snow many a winter day to fire up the old furnace early and have the school warm for the students when they arrived. They don't make them like Pop any more. He was quite a guy.

19

The Day I Saw Dogs Dancing

CAUTION: This chapter is rated "PG-13" for reasons that will be obvious when you read it (if you can't guess from the title).

One day while riding my bike along Wright Street a couple of blocks from home, I came upon something I'd never seen before. It was the weirdest thing I'd ever witnessed up to that point in my young life. What I saw were two dogs "dancing" together in the middle of the street. One dog was on all fours and the other one was up on its hind legs sort of leaning on the other one from behind. As they jerked and jumped around and around in circles, the one on all fours was twisting its head back and growling and snapping at the one on two legs. The one in back was howling as if in pain. They looked like they were somehow stuck together. And to make matters worse, a lady was smacking at them with a broom while several kids stood on the sidewalk nearby laughing at the whole situation. I just sat there on my bike staring in disbelief at what I was seeing. Several questions came to my mind: *What the heck's going on here? Is this really happening? What are those crazy dogs doing?*

Finally, after several minutes, the dogs suddenly separated and ran off in opposite directions. The lady with the broom chased after the dog that had been on the bottom and yelled, "Get home, Missy!" The other dog kept running down the street and was never seen again. The broom lady headed for a nearby house and seemed satisfied that she'd helped the dogs out of their predicament. The kids followed her inside. I rode on home in amazement and decided I'd ask my father about what I'd just seen. He was raised in the country around animals and would likely know what those two dogs were doing.

After Dad got home from work and we had supper, I cornered him out on the front porch reading the newspaper. The girls were helping Mom with the dishes, so it was just him and me. I said, "Dad, I gotta ask you about something really strange I saw this afternoon." I then proceeded to describe in great detail the two dancing dogs. As I finished my description, a smile came across Dad's face and he laughed. He thought for a few seconds, then said, "Yes, that sure was a strange sight to see. It doesn't happen too often. I've seen dogs doing that several times over the years. Let me try to explain what was going on."

Dad then launched into one of his unforgettable explanations. "You see, son, boy dogs like to get on top of girl dogs at certain times. And when they do they, uh, stick their weenie in the girl dog's hind end under her tail. It looks like it's going in the girl dog's butt, but it's really going into another hole that puppies come out of when they're born. Once in a while, if the boy dog is a little too big for the girl dog they get stuck together and the boy dog can't pull out. When I was a kid, we used to call it a 'dog knot.' Why, I can remember once when I was about your age seeing two dogs like that who couldn't get apart for almost an hour."

An hour? My eyes must have bulged at the thought of such a thing happening. I sat there in stunned silence at what I'd just heard. Dad asked me if I had any other questions about what I'd seen. I did. "Well, why was the lady beating them with a broom?"

He replied, "It may have looked like she was hurting them, but she was actually trying to help them get apart. When two dogs like that can't get separated on their own, you sometimes have to throw a bucket of water on them or turn a hose on them to cool them down. Since she didn't have any water nearby, she probably grabbed her broom and thought she'd give them something else to think about."

All I could say was, "Good golly."

Dad looked at me and smiled again. He wrapped up his explanation by saying, "I know this may all seem a little hard to understand at your age, but I'll talk to you more about it someday soon and explain how it works with men and women when they make babies."

If what I saw those two dogs doing was weird, Dad's overly detailed explanation of it was even weirder to the innocent ears of a naive twelve-and-a-half year old. We didn't have sex education in the schools back then. Sooner or later, most boys received a little talk about "the birds and the bees" from their fathers, and I guess girls received a similar talk from their mothers. Younger kids also picked up sexual information—and misinformation—from older kids. In my case it was eventually a combination of both.

I hadn't yet received my official parental introduction to the wonderful world of sex. But if it was anything like what those dogs were doing, I wasn't at all sure that I wanted to know more about it—let alone ever *do* it. The very thought of it seemed nasty and disgusting. With my overactive boyish imagination I could just see myself with some girl in such an awkward position while her angry mother beat on me with a broom and her even angrier father threw a bucket of water on us. It was *not* a pretty picture. I secretly vowed it would *never* happen to me.

This early visual experience and the resulting horror story from my father probably played a major role in my remaining a virgin until after I was married—or maybe it was the lack of opportunities. I have to admit that, after I later learned the so-called "facts of life" from Dad and my hormones started kicking in, I did come close to doing what comes naturally a few times while a teenager. But, whenever I'd start descending into the dark depths of passion, I'd think about dog knots and my urges subsided rather quickly before being acted upon—and without anyone hitting me with a broom or throwing water on us.

20

Ha-Ha-Ha-Ye!

During my grade school years while growing up on Wright Street, I'd occasionally hear a curious shout off in the distance. An unknown boy's voice—not always the same boy—would yell out, "Ha-ha-ha-ye!" Usually, I'd then hear another boy holler back the same strange syllables from even farther away. I never knew who these boys were or what the meaning was of their mysterious call to one another. But it was so odd that it stuck in my mind after hearing it several times over the years.

One Saturday, I walked around the corner from my house to collect from a nearby customer on my paper route. Way down Sanders Street, I saw two boys approaching. Suddenly, from their direction came that unusual cry: "Ha-ha-ha-ye!" I looked around and didn't see anyone else, so figured they had directed it at me. Without even thinking, I raised my hands to my mouth and immediately called back, "Ha-ha-ha-ye!"

The sound had barely left my mouth when I noticed the two boys had started running toward me. As they grew closer, I didn't recognize them from the neighborhood or from my school. They may have been from the other side of East Street or Catholics who went to Saint Patrick's. As they ran up to me, I could tell from the looks on their faces that they didn't know me either—and didn't want to.

One of the boys—the taller of the two—said, "Hey, kid. Where do you live and what do you mean by yelling that back at us? Are you trying to be a smart-ass?"

I didn't know what to say, so I simply told them the truth. "Uh, I live around the corner on Wright Street and I've heard other kids yelling that back and forth. So, when you yelled it at me, I thought I was supposed to answer you by yelling it back. That's all."

The shorter boy obviously didn't like my response and sneered at me when he said, "Well you can't go around yelling that unless you're in our club. It's *our* secret call. If you ever use it again you'll be sorry. Really sorry."

That sounded like a threat, which I'm sure it was. Even though they didn't say *why* I'd regret doing it and gave me no specific details of the dire consequences that might result, I got their message loud and clear. "I'm sorry. I didn't know what it meant. I won't ever do it again." My apology and promise seemed to satisfy them. I could tell because Shorty now had a smug look on his face instead of a sneer.

"Well, okay. But remember what we said." The big boy nodded to emphasize his buddy's words. He wasn't sneering and he looked almost friendly. The idea flickered through my mind that maybe they'd invite me to join their club, but, of course, no such invitation was offered. And I sure didn't feel like it was a very good time to inquire about membership opportunities.

I wish I could've learned more about their club, like who was in it, what they called it, and what ha-ha-ha-ye meant. It sounded really neat to be in such a group and have your own special identification call for use by members only. I thought again for a second that maybe if I asked them about joining, they might be open to the idea. But I just stood there like a bump on a log and didn't dare say another word.

The tall boy passed me on my right, Shorty passed me on my left, and they went on their way up Sanders toward Fountain Square. I looked over my shoulder to make sure they weren't going to pull a sneak attack when they got behind me. But they didn't and, boy, was I glad. I was never a fighter anyway, and with two against one, I wouldn't have had a prayer.

So, I never became a member of that secret club and, with the exception of this single "illegal" incident, never again yelled that mystical call down the street at another boy. I was darn lucky I didn't get beat up because of my one-time act of ignorance. Any time after that whenever I heard a boy call out "Ha-ha-ha-ye!" I just kept my mouth shut and went on about my business. But I still wished I knew what the heck that crazy-sounding call word meant. I guess some things in life are meant to remain a secret. And this was one of them.

TRUE CONFESSION: Actually, I *did* yell out this cry one other time. As I was going up to my bedroom one day, I passed the window on the stairway landing. Looking down, I saw a boy I didn't know walking along the alley beside our house. He didn't see me peeking out the window as he called "Ha-ha-ha-ye!" at some other kid he must have spotted down the alley. I listened, but he received no answer. I waited until he was well past our house, then quietly opened the window. Using my hands as a makeshift megaphone, I yelled out "Ha-ha-ha-ye!", then quickly closed the window. He never knew where my answering call came from. I laughed to myself, satisfied that I'd put one over on him.

21

First Date Ever

Kids in my day were like today's young people when it came to dating: some started earlier than others. I was among those who began participating in this social custom earlier than most of my friends. I asked a girl out on my first date ever while I was still in grade school. I was an eighth-grader just about ready to graduate from Abraham Lincoln Elementary School #18 and venture into the world of high school.

Crossing the dividing line that separated those who'd never had a date from those who had wasn't easy. It took a very special girl to make me want to cross that invisible line, and that girl was Dorothy Muse. She was really pretty, a year or so younger than me, and a classmate of my sister, Sandy. They say you never forget the first time you do anything in your life. And I have vivid memories of my date with Dorothy, although not just for the expected reasons.

Our date was in the middle of winter when it was "colder than snot" as kids used to say. I don't recall the details of how or when I got up the nerve to ask Dorothy to the movies; the important thing I do remember was that she said yes and we were going. Since I was still way too young to drive, my father acted as our chauffeur. After church and Sunday dinner, Dad drove me over to Dorothy's house on Iowa Street. She lived on a hillside that required climbing a steep flight of at least a dozen steps to reach her front door. I made the ascent, rang the doorbell, and stood there catching my breath.

A moment later Dorothy answered the door and welcomed me in. Her house was toasty warm and I was glad to get inside out of the freezing air. She introduced me to her folks and I shook hands with her father in a display of my best manners. They asked me what movie we were going to see and where it was playing. I told them the details and added that my father was driving us there. Dorothy got her coat and I helped her on with it. We said our goodbyes and made our way down the long set of steps to the street where Dad was waiting in the car.

Of course, I was more than a little nervous as I introduced Dad to Dorothy and was secretly thankful that he was along to help carry the conversation. Dad drove up Shelby Street to the Fountain Square Theatre and let us out right in front. I didn't make any arrangements with him to pick us up—a major mistake as it turned out. I'd already told him that I wanted to walk Dorothy home after the movies. She lived about a mile away from the theater. It wouldn't have been a bad walk in nice weather, but in the dead of winter it was going to be a long, cold trek indeed. But I'm getting ahead of myself.

For the first time in my life, I went up to the lady in the ticket booth and proudly said (a little louder than necessary), "TWO, please." The main attraction was the new hit movie *Tammy* featuring the popular up-and-coming starlet Debbie Reynolds. This was way back when she was just a teenager (or young enough to still look like one). As we entered the lobby, I asked Dorothy if she'd like something from the concession stand. She surprised me when she said that she didn't care for anything. I had plenty of money with me (thanks to my paper route earnings) and would have bought her whatever she wanted. Since she wasn't having anything, I didn't want to sit there and eat in front of her, so I skipped my usual roll of Necco Wafers.

The show hadn't started yet and we found seats on the main floor several rows back under the balcony (I wanted to make sure we'd be safe from anything tossed off by any pranksters who might be upstairs). After sitting there for a few minutes in our heavy coats, we quickly became overheated and decided to take them off.

It was then that I really noticed even in the dim light how well-developed Dorothy was for her age. I'd noticed "them" before at school, but had never been this close to her. Her Ban-Lon sweater only emphasized their bulging presence. Oh, boy!

Helping Dorothy off with her coat required me to put my arm up around her shoulders. It was a nice feeling that I immediately decided I wanted more of. I also discovered that in addition to looking good, Dorothy smelled good—*really* good. So, after adjusting her coat, I ever-so-slowly-and-carefully inched my arm up across the top of her seat back and left it there. She didn't seem to notice and, if she did, she made no objection. After ten or fifteen minutes, I finally decided to be daring and move my arm down from the seat back and place it directly around her shoulders.

This seemed like a great idea, but turned into a major problem. Not because she objected to it (she didn't), but because my arm had "fallen asleep" from resting on the hard edge of her seat back and it went numb on me. Pins and needles started shooting through my hand and I finally had to withdraw my arm to flex it a few times and wiggle and rub my fingers to restore feeling in them. Imagine trying to do that without being obvious about it. I was afraid Dorothy might think I was having some kind of a fit or a seizure, but she didn't seem to notice my unusual movements. After this unexpected setback, I lost my nerve completely and didn't try putting my arm back around her the whole time we were there.

In those days, boys and girls didn't kiss on the first date—at least that's what I'd been led to believe. Dorothy was *not* considered an "easy" girl and, since I was totally inexperienced in dating (and in kissing), I wasn't willing to risk a slap in the face by being too bold. So, we just sat there side by side quite properly and watched Tammy and her adventures. No hand-holding, no hugging, no kissing. But, remember, this wasn't just my first date with Dorothy, it was my very first date *ever* with *any* girl. This was also possibly her first date ever. We were just a couple of beginners who still had much to learn.

During the entire double-feature (I don't even remember what the second movie was) and all the other stuff that went along with it, neither Dorothy nor I left our seats. We hardly said two words to one another because in those days people didn't talk during the movies. People around us would have said, "Shhhh!" or called an usher to reprimand us.

The show finally ended and we stood up to put on our coats. I was almost stiff from sitting for nearly four hours without moving. Dorothy likely felt the same. Those double features were killers. As we walked up the aisle to the lobby, I was proud to be walking beside Dorothy and hoped the feeling was mutual. You might know, there wasn't a single kid from school to see us and start the buzz that Charles took Dorothy to the movies on a date. Maybe it was just as well the way things turned out.

As we came to the lobby, Dorothy told me in a quiet voice that she wanted to go upstairs a minute before we started home. I didn't catch what she meant at first, but then it dawned on me that the restrooms were upstairs. I said, "Oh, okay, sure." I told her that I'd meet her right there in the lobby near the foot of the stairway. Instead of doing the smart thing and going up to the restroom myself (although I really didn't feel much like I needed to go), I just stood there and waited on her to return. After she'd gone upstairs, I *almost* decided to do likewise. But I didn't because she now had a head start on me and might get back before I would. Since I'd already promised to meet her in the lobby, if I wasn't standing there when she returned, I was afraid she might think I'd ran out on her. Unrealistic? Yes. But so worked the mind of an inexperienced boy who wasn't quite fourteen on his first date.

A few minutes later, Dorothy came down the stairway. She smiled when she saw me standing at the bottom; I smiled up at her. Waiting on her there had been worth it just to see that smile. As she descended, I appreciated just how pretty she really was and how lucky I was to be on a date with her. My previous silly concern and any thought about my own personal comfort instantly disappeared. After buttoning up our coats and pulling on our gloves, we ventured out into what had become a cloudy, gray, late afternoon. Believe me, after sitting in an overly warm theater for a few hours, the contrast in temperature was really noticeable, not to mention uncomfortable. Brrr!

Being a gentleman, I remembered to stay on the curb side as we walked along braving the frigid wind gusting down Shelby Street. Luckily, the wind was to our backs and not in our faces. We both stood our coat collars up around our necks. Dorothy wrapped her long woolen scarf over her ears. I wasn't wearing a hat, so pulled out my furry earmuffs and stuck them on (yes, kids wore earmuffs in those days—even the boys). I awkwardly took her gloved hand in mind and our fingers interlocked as we hurried down the street. I wasn't trying to get romantic or anything, it just seemed the thing to do in the brisk wind.

In a short time our cheeks grew stiff from the cold. This, along with our teeth being on the verge of chattering, made it a real trick to carry on much of a conversation, but we managed the best we could as we hurried along. Her voice had a bit of a Kentucky-southern accent that I thought was really cute. I could have listened to it forever—but not under these conditions. Since I had earmuffs on and the wind was blowing, I had to listen intently to hear her. We both had to raise our voices a little while we talked some about the movie, about school, and a few other things that kids in those days were interested in.

Then, my trouble began. I don't know if it was something I'd eaten for dinner, or if it was nervousness, or the extreme cold—probably a combination of all three—but it seemed like every block we walked my need to pee became stronger and stronger. At first it was just a subtle reminder in the back of my mind, then it became an urge, then a demand, and finally it became an impossible-to-ignore cry for help from my bladder. I though it was going to burst. Ever try to carry on a casual conversation with a girl when you feel like you're about to wet your pants? It wasn't easy, but with superhuman effort I somehow managed. Dorothy didn't suspect a thing—at least I hoped she didn't. Why hadn't I been smart enough to go before I left the theater when I had the chance? After all, Dorothy hadn't been ashamed to say she needed to go upstairs to the restroom. I realized how stupid I'd been not to do likewise. And, now, with every step, I was paying the price for my mistake.

We finally arrived at Dorothy's house—with me still trying not to walk funny and make it obvious that I was in distress. As we reached the bottom of that long set of steps up to her front porch, she invited me in for some hot chocolate. Did I take her up on her offer, so I could use the bathroom, thaw out, and get to know her better? Oh, no. Not me. By now my mind was so focused on the urgency of needing to relieve myself that it was all I could think about. So, instead of accepting her invitation, I made up a lame excuse about how I had to get home and finish some homework for school the next day. A boy will say anything in an emergency to save face in front of a girl he's trying to impress.

We parted there on the sidewalk. It was a good thing we did because I don't think I could've made it up all those steps. I stood there watching as she climbed the hillside to her porch. She turned and we waved to one another as she went inside. I tried to walk on down the street normally in case she was watching from a window—as if she would really be watching me walk away. Dream on!

Anyway, as soon as I turned the corner and was out of sight of her house, I took off running for home as fast as I dared under the circumstances. My house was about a mile away and my need to go grew so strong that I had serious doubts about whether I was going to make it or not. And there were no public restrooms along the way; it was an all-residential area. Running may have shortened my travel time, but the bouncing up and down while I ran only intensified my pain. The closer I got to home, the more certain I became that I *wasn't* going to make it in time. I held on with all my strength even though the pain in my abdomen was nearly unbearable.

Then, at last, I made it—but only by the skin of my teeth. As I stormed in the front door, my lungs were burning from sucking in so much cold air and my bladder was in pure agony because I'd held myself so long. Without stopping or hardly speaking to my folks, I peeled off my gloves, unbuttoned my coat, and headed straight for our one and only bathroom, taking the most direct route through their bedroom. Thank heavens no one was occupying the throne in my time of urgent need. To my great surprise, as I stood there and stood there trying to go, I discovered that I *couldn't* go. I'd tensed myself up so tightly and held it for so long that my muscles wouldn't relax. After standing there for a couple of minutes and relaxing a little, I finally let go—and I peed like a horse. I'm sure my parents could hear me through the thin bathroom door. But I didn't care. I'd found sweet relief.

After draining myself, I took off my coat and warmed up by standing over the kitchen register. I remembered to straddle it and not stand directly on the metal grate so I wouldn't melt the rubber heels on my shoes. The warmth felt wonderful as it came up inside the legs of my corduroy trousers. Aaah!

When I was thawed out and able to enjoy the restored comfort of a now empty bladder, I went into the living room. My parents naturally asked me how my date with Dorothy went. And, of course, I said nothing at all about the near disaster of waddling down Shelby Street, then dashing home, and nearly peeing my pants. They probably guessed what had happened by my panicked entry and immediate beeline for the bathroom when I returned. If that didn't tip them off, then the hard-to-ignore sound of my high-pressure, high-volume splashing no doubt confirmed it.

I never found out if Dorothy really enjoyed—or didn't enjoy—our date. I figured it must not have gone too badly, at least not from her point of view. Why? Well, she did let me hold her hand all the way to her house. Even though we had on heavy wool gloves, I still enjoyed the experience. And she had also invited me in once we got there. Maybe she wasn't just being polite and maybe she really had wanted me to come in for a while. Unfortunately, I would never know.

I only had a few more days at School #18 and was busy with end-of-semester and graduation activities. Then, school was out for the Christmas-New Year's vacation. I started to

Manual High School right after the holiday break (as one of those mid-term grade school graduates who began in January). As a result of all this, I never saw Dorothy or spoke to her again. Even though I'd really enjoyed being with her on our date, my crazy "bladder control" problem had been so traumatic that I just wanted to put the whole experience behind me. And that meant never dating her again. Besides, after entering high school, I thought it wouldn't be cool to date a lowly grade-schooler. That made a convenient excuse to never call her. What a heel!

I'm not sure whatever happened to Dorothy. She may have moved away to another school district because I don't remember ever seeing her at Manual. But I do know that I still—even now—regret the way things turned out on that cold wintry afternoon so many years ago. Dorothy will always occupy a unique place in my memory and in my heart as the very first girl I ever took on a date.

On rare occasions through the years, I've heard that old familiar theme song from *Tammy* played on the radio. And each time I hear it, I remember a pretty young girl named Dorothy and a dumb boy who wasn't even smart enough to go to the bathroom when he should've. I also think about what *might* have been . . . if only . . . if only . . .

Dorothy, I know this is really a long shot, but if you're out there somewhere (and I sincerely hope that you are) and read this story, please contact me. I'd love to hear what you thought about our date. Also, I owe you a super-big apology that I'm ready and willing to make—even after all these years.

22

And Bingo Was His Name

One evening as we were finishing supper, Dad asked me and my two sisters an unexpected question. "What would you kids think about getting a dog?" Although we'd brought up the idea a few times over the years, I didn't remember any of us asking for a dog recently and was puzzled about what motivated Dad to bring up the subject. Nevertheless, my sisters were immediately excited about such a possibility and eagerly expressed their desire to have one. I, on the other hand, was far less enthused because I felt certain, since I was both the oldest child and the only boy in the family, that most of the responsibility of caring for a dog would fall on me.

I reluctantly said I guessed it would be okay to have a dog, but that I thought all three of us kids should share *equally* in taking care of it. Dad agreed fully and said that sharing the responsibility was an absolute requirement for us to have one. My sisters, of course, both pledged to take turns in any dog-related duties. But, somehow, I doubted the depth and endurance of their commitment.

The next question was what kind of dog we should get. After a short discussion of a few popular breeds, the three of us agreed on a cocker spaniel. And we wanted a blond one. Mom was mostly silent during our deliberation. I sensed that she was not so much in favor of getting a dog. After all, we already had not one, but two, parakeets. And we'd also gone through the experience of raising two baby squirrels that blew into our backyard during a bad summer storm. Raising them as pets was probably the main reason she wasn't excited about getting a dog. There were certain characteristics about four-legged animals that did not endear them to our mother. They can bite and scratch. They chew on things they shouldn't. They can be messy. And they sometimes smell. On top of that, dogs shed hair. Despite her misgivings, she was outvoted and the decision was made: we would get a dog and it would be a blond cocker spaniel.

I was more than a little surprised that Dad accepted our choice without argument. I thought he might just want us to go to the city dog pound and get a "Heinz 57" mutt. Instead, he said he'd check the newspaper and try to locate a full-blooded cocker. After a few days of searching the classified advertisements, Dad found an ad for a litter of blond cocker puppies. He called the number listed and the man selling them said they'd recently been weaned and he had three left. The price was a no-haggle $50. This was a considerable sum back in 1955. The man said he was selling the pups on a first-come, first-served basis. So, Dad told him we'd be there the next day around 5:30 pm to pick out our puppy.

We could hardly wait till the appointed time. Even I was growing mildly excited about getting a pup. And I didn't get excited very easily or often. The next evening, when Dad came home from work, we all piled into our Nash Ambassador and headed to the address in the newspaper ad.

When we arrived, the dog man said he still had the three puppies: two males and a female. Dad favored a female because he thought it would be gentler around us kids. But we didn't care about its gender, as long as it was a blond cocker spaniel.

The man led us behind his house to a large pen where two of the three pups were running around and playing with each another. The third one just sat there by itself and looked at us in kind of a pathetic "please take me" way. My sisters and I took a careful look at all three dogs, then agreed instantly and unanimously on the one we wanted. We all cried—almost in unison—"We want *that* one." The pup we favored was the loner. It was a male and had a slightly flattened muzzle which we thought gave him a cuter look than the other two. Even though Dad had favored a female, he went along with our choice.

The dog man said, "I figured he'd be the hardest one to sell because of his nose. It doesn't meet the judging standards for cockers. Their noses are supposed to be a little longer and more pointed." Dad said that was okay because we just wanted him for a family pet and we wouldn't be entering him in any dog shows. The man looked at us kids and saw our excitement over getting the pup we'd chosen. Then, he told Dad, "I'll tell you what. Since you're going to give the pup a good home you can have him for $30. I wouldn't feel right charging the full price for a snub-nose. How's that sound?"

Dad thanked him and counted out the money while Mom looked on as if thinking of other things we could have used it for. The man entered the pen and after a few tries grabbed up the scampering puppy we'd chosen. He came over and handed the pup, not to Dad or to Mom, but to me. I had to admit the little guy was awfully cute as I cuddled him, although I didn't care much for him licking my face with his slobbery wet tongue.

We all climbed into the car and put the dog on the floor. We'd brought some old bath towels and spread them over the rear floor mats just in case the new puppy had any "accidents" on our way home. It turned out to be a wise precaution. The pup hadn't been in the car five minutes until he peed. It was a sign of things to come.

On the way home, my sisters and I took turns petting our new puppy and trying to keep him as calm as possible while Dad was driving. Mom asked us what we thought would be a good name for the dog. This started a debate on the merits of several suggestions. None of them caught our fancy until one of the girls—I think it was Sandy—came up with a winner. She said they'd recently sung a cute song in her music class about a dog. She remembered a line from the song went, ". . . and Bingo was his name." Sandy asked, "How about calling him Bingo?" Jackie and I both thought this was the perfect name. When you looked at him, he just seemed like a dog that ought to be called Bingo.

As soon as we got back home, we turned Bingo loose in our big backyard. Since the yard was surrounded by a chain-link fence, we didn't have to worry about him running off. Dad reminded us to be sure and keep both the gates closed and latched properly at all times. We promised that we would. Dad told me to get a bowl and fill it with water in case Bingo was thirsty. When he ran over to investigate the bowl and started lapping up some water, we saw an immediate problem. Cockers have fairly long ears that hang down. When he stuck his face in the water bowl his ears hung into the water. Dad made a note to buy a special dog dish with tapered sides to help solve Bingo's ears-in-the-water problem.

After watching Bingo running around sniffing at everything for a few more minutes, we all went inside and washed up for supper. By now it was well past our regular meal time and we were good and hungry. After we ate, the girls helped Mom clean up the table and do the dishes. Dad and I went out to see how Bingo was doing. He must have worn himself out running around so much because he was lying on his belly panting. Since we hadn't yet bought any regular dog food, we gave Bingo some finely cut-up pieces of meat left over from supper. He nibbled at them slowly at first, then gobbled down the rest without even chewing them. Dad gave me some money and made me responsible for buying a few cans of dog food at Fisher's Market the next day.

Bingo was going to be a house dog, not a yard dog. So, the next problem we faced was where he was going to be kept when he was inside. Since he wasn't housebroken, Mom was dead set against him having free run of the whole house. Dad agreed and came up with a solution. When he was in the house, Bingo would be confined to the short hallway running from the kitchen, past the bathroom, to the doorway leading up to my bedroom. The hall had a linoleum floor which would make it easy to clean up any accidents—which we knew were bound to happen. There was a door at the far end of the hall and another into the bathroom, but there was no door at the kitchen end of the hallway.

Dad quickly improvised a barricade out of a large piece of corrugated cardboard which he propped up against the door frame with one of our kitchen chairs. It was a bit of a hassle having to step over the cardboard barrier every time any of us—mostly me—went up and down the hallway, but we soon got used to it. Dad had me cover the hallway floor with old newspapers. This seemed like a good idea, but turned out to be a mistake. Bingo took great delight in grabbing the sheets of paper in his mouth and tearing them to pieces. We soon decided that maybe we didn't need the newspaper after all. Whenever Bingo peed in his hallway confinement area, we just wiped it up off the linoleum—and the sooner the better so it wouldn't leave a stain.

Mom definitely didn't want Bingo on the living room carpet—this was the only room in our house that had a nearly room-size rug. After he was finally housebroken, she gave in on that restriction and Bingo had the run of the entire house. I don't remember him ever coming up into my bedroom, however; I guess he didn't like climbing all those steps. They were fairly steep.

Much to Mom's dismay, Bingo occasionally had an episode of itchy butt and would perform his infamous "roop scoot" across the living room carpet at the most unexpected times, usually when we had company. We kids always found it really funny, but Mom thought it was nasty and embarrassing and made us take Bingo outside whenever he did it. Luckily, the living room carpet was dark brown, so no skid marks showed after Mom dutifully cleaned up any traces left by Bingo's naughty tricks. Like any male dog, he also liked to hump an occasional leg—and he didn't care whose it was. Any leg would do. This also brought lots of giggles to us kids, unless it was *our* leg being attacked.

As I'd feared when the idea of getting a dog was first proposed, the burden of taking care of Bingo eventually fell almost entirely on me. Oh, sure, the girls helped some at first, but little by little my share of the work became greater and greater. Whenever he went out in the yard to do his business, it was my unpleasant task to clean up his poop. I always hated doing that. Whenever it was rainy and the grass was wet, I also had to thoroughly towel-dry Bingo so he wouldn't make a wet mess in the house. That's when I discovered firsthand that wet dogs smell bad. He also had doggie breath a lot of the time. My squeamish sisters missed out on these special joys I had while caring for our dog.

Winter time brought additional duties.

Bingo had long hair that would drag through the snow on his toileting trips into the backyard. If there was much snow at all, his belly hair would drag through it and he ended up with a lot of little ice balls hanging from his underside. Trying to pull these off his hair was no fun—and Bingo didn't like it much either. To solve this seasonal problem, I took scissors and trimmed back the hair on his tummy. Presto! Problem solved. I was tired of cleaning up his wet paw prints from the back door across the kitchen floor. So, I also trimmed some of the hair from around his paws to make them easier to dry off.

The girls did occasionally help out a little by keeping Bingo's water bowl full and putting out his food at the appointed times. But whenever they "forgot," I ended up doing it. Everything else—all the unpleasant jobs—fell on me. Despite these inconveniences, Bingo was cute even after he grew up and we all loved him. Sometimes, we'd dress him up in an old T-shirt, which he seemed to enjoy wearing around the house. Mom warmed up to Bingo and bought him a little red wool doggie sweater which he could wear outside in the winter. But wrestling him into the tight-fitting garment was more trouble than it was worth for his brief forays into the cold. We soon gave up on making him wear it.

I can't remember ever taking Bingo for a

walk; I don't think we even owned a leash. He got plenty of exercise running around in our backyard. Bingo matured into a healthy dog. The only time he went to the vet was to get "fixed" and to have his tail bobbed, plus to update his shots. We had him during high school and beyond. Over the next few years, my sisters and I graduated from high school. We were married one-by-one and moved out to make our own lives. Bingo stayed behind with Dad and Mom and we'd see him whenever we visited them, usually at least once a week since we all lived in the neighborhood.

One day, Joyce (now pregnant and really showing it) and I stopped by my folk's house for a brief visit. As soon as we got inside, it was obvious that Bingo wasn't around because he always ran into the living room when any visitors came in. I figured he was out in the backyard and asked, "Where's Bingo?" Silence. Dad looked down at the floor like he didn't want to answer me. Mom finally spoke up and said, "Your father got rid of him." I could tell by the sharp tone of her voice that she didn't agree with his decision. Dad finally spoke up, "Aw, Evelyn. I just didn't want him around with their baby coming."

Mom told me years later that after having his first heart attack, certain parts of Dad's personality had changed and he'd turned against having a dog. Maybe he thought that with us kids grown and gone, and his health not being good, having Bingo around would become a burden for Mom to take care of alone. He was right about that. Mom had gradually grown tired of the dog after my sisters and I left home one by one. In any case, a few days prior to our visit, they had taken Bingo to "an agency that finds good homes for pets whose owners no longer want them or can no longer keep them." I didn't inquire further, but felt sure they were talking about the city dog pound.

My sisters and I were all living in rental housing at the time. None of the places allowed pets. My sister, Sandy, told me later that she and her husband, Dick, would have even considered moving out of their apartment in order to have taken Bingo. But, it was too late. Bingo was gone.

We tried to console ourselves by thinking that since he was so cute he surely would have been adopted quickly by someone else. On the other hand, he was an older dog, had gotten overweight, and wasn't quite as cute as he had been in his younger days. We all knew the pound only kept animals so long, and we didn't want to think about the alternative if Bingo wasn't adopted. As a result, none of us had the nerve to check and see what became of him. I don't know if the pound people would have told us if he had been put down or not. But we preferred to believe that Bingo was now in a good home somewhere with new owners. If not, we consoled ourselves by believing that he surely must have gone to Doggie Heaven.

I'll always remember him as a good dog. He never bit anyone or tore up anything of value and he provided us kids with lots of laughs at his funny tricks—even the naughty ones. We all loved him and we knew he loved us. Yes, he was a good old dog. And Bingo was his name.

Me holding Bingo as a pup out in our backyard shortly after he became part of our family.

Full-grown Bingo in his wool sweater (which he seldom wore because it was such a hassle getting him into it).

23

Taking the Giant Step

After completing my elementary education at Abraham Lincoln School #18, I was ready to take the next giant step in my life: starting to high school. Kids graduating from P. S. #18 and several other south side grade schools were all funneled into Manual High School. My mother had graduated from Manual in the Class of 1937, so she was glad that I would attend the same high school she had.

Manual had a long history since it was the second oldest high school in Indianapolis (only Shortridge was older). Started in 1884 as High School No. 2, the school was housed in an eight-room addition built on to P. S. #8 on Virginia Avenue. In 1895, the high school moved into a much larger new facility located on South Meridian Street just a block below South Street. At that time, the school was renamed the Industrial Training School. The school became known as the Manual Training School in 1899. Then, in 1916, the school was renamed Emmerich Manual Training High School in honor of Charles E. Emmerich, the first principal back when it was originally known as the Industrial Training School. Technically, the school should have become known as Emmerich after that, but instead it was referred to by its students and the community as Manual. And it has remained so ever since.

Manual was located on a five-sided tract of land bordered by Henry Street on the north, South Meridian Street on the east, and Russell Avenue on the west. The land came to a point on its southern end where Meridian and Russell merged. Merrill Street ran east-west through the middle of the property. An enclosed bridge spanned the street to connect the original main building with a later addition (opened in 1922) housing a cafeteria, gymnasium, and auditorium. This may have been the first such building-to-building connecting bridge in the city.

Manual was built mostly of red bricks with limestone trim. The main part of the building stood four stories tall; other parts stepped down to three and two stories. The center portion of the building had two distinctive square towers. At one time they may have included bells or chimes, but if so I never heard them. Some sections of the building's outer walls became covered with ivy planted by various graduating classes over the decades. Because of this, the school's yearbook was called *The Ivian*. At Manual, that nostalgic old song "The Halls of Ivy" was second in popularity only to the rousing school song, "Onward, Manual!" which was set to the well-known tune of "On, Wisconsin," famous fight song of that university.

I was what they called a mid-term graduate from elementary school and began attending Manual in January of 1953. At that time a modern new facility was under construction to house the high school much further south at the corner of Madison Avenue and Pleasant Run Parkway. The south side of the city was growing and needed a larger facility for the increasing number of high school students. Not so much at the time, but later, I felt fortunate to have attended one semester at what would soon become known as "old Manual" (later renamed Harry E. Wood High School). Taking classes in the historic old facility made me really appreciate the new one when it opened. I sometimes wish that all incoming Manual students could have had the same opportunity that I had of attending both the old and the new school.

The first day of the winter semester was cold, but clear; so I rode my bicycle to Manual. The school was only about a mile away from where I lived (a distance easily walked), but I had to hurry home after school because while a "fresh-freshman" I still had an afternoon paper route. The school building had a special door on the Meridian Street side for bicyclists to enter. I arrived early and the door wasn't unlocked yet. So, I had to wait outside for about ten minutes. Several other riders soon began arriving. When the door was finally unlocked and swung open by the custodian, I was first in line and eager to get in out of the cold—just a little too eager. Having never before entered the building, I didn't know what I was getting into. It turned out there was a fairly steep ramp downward from the sidewalk-level door to the floor of the basement. I went *riding* in not expecting a slope. The ramp and the floor were both smoothly finished concrete and were very slick. I quickly applied my bike's coaster brake and skidded down the ramp, onto the floor level, and nearly crashed into a wall before I got the bike under control. The custodian yelled at me, "Hey, kid. Don't you know you're supposed to *walk* your bike down the ramp?" No, I didn't know. But I learned fast—the hard way. All the other boys, who were properly walking their bikes down the ramp behind me, were laughing like crazy. I quickly dismounted and walked my bike over to the racks provided. My face was no doubt bright red, more from my total embarrassment than from the cold. What a way to start my first day in high school.

Entering the boy's dimly lighted locker room, I found my way through the huge maze of lockers until I located the one assigned to me. I'd brought my own padlock (as instructed) and was careful not to make the foolish mistake of locking my key inside the locker. Sticking my school satchel under my arm, I rubbed my still-cold cheeks as I headed off to find my first classroom. The adventure had begun. I was now officially in high school.

Since Manual had several floor levels, a lot of stair-climbing was required. My mother had warned me on my first day not to fall victim to any upperclassmen who might try to sell me a so-called "elevator pass" because *there were no elevators*. In any case, no such bogus passes were offered to me by anyone. It must have been an old trick that they used to pull back in her days at Manual. Some of my classes were widely separated in the building and I really had to hustle to get to them on time. Manual, I quickly discovered, was way bigger than School #18. Way, way bigger.

I lucked out and had a really neat teacher for my English class. Her last name escapes me, but her first name was Nancy. She told us we could call her by her first name—a drastic departure from the usual practice of using last names only. Nancy was young and sort of a tomboy; she had short hair with bangs and wore slacks instead of dresses. She also played the harmonica and would sometimes favor us with a tune at the beginning of class. I know it sounds corny, but we enjoyed it. She made learning fun. She was also cute in an unusual sort of way. Soon, many of the boys in my class—including me—had crushes on her.

Another Manual memory that's related to the one just shared is about attending, of all things, square dancing classes. Why I would ever participate in these is beyond me; I never was much of a dancer. My probable motivation was that it would be a good way to meet and get to know some girls. And, believe me, there were *lots* of them to meet. Another powerful attracting factor was that the sponsor of these classes was Nancy, the popular and likeable English teacher I previously mentioned. Most of us boys likely signed up just for the opportunity to be around her more.

Anyway, I can remember stumbling my way through the classes (I was born with the proverbial "two left feet"), all the while in the back of my mind thinking, *This square dancing is really dumb.* But I did get to hold girl's hands and put my arm around their waist, so it was worth the suffering I had to endure for this exciting privilege. The only problem was that some of the girls who took the classes were not ones I really wanted to put my arm around or whose hands I wanted to hold. But I learned a valuable lesson: sometimes you have to take the bad with the good. I did meet some cute girls. So, overall, I guess it was an okay experience.

Sadly, when we began our next semester in the new facility, we discovered that there was no more Nancy. Perhaps her short haircut, slacks, and harmonica were just a bit too unorthodox and she may have been considered by those in positions of power as too far ahead of her time. Maybe she only had a temporary contract to fill in for a teacher who was out of school having a baby. I don't know, but in any case, we never saw her again. I wondered where she ended up teaching and what lucky kids had her for English—and maybe for square dancing. She sure was cute. And she could really play a mean harmonica.

I was never an athletic-type and didn't enjoy having to take the mandatory physical education classes at Manual. My gym teacher that first semester was the dreaded Mr. Alvin Romeiser, a tough old guy with a husky voice and a big jaw that looked like he could bite nails in two if he felt like it. His face had a nut-brown complexion full of wrinkles and was crowned with white hair that he wore in a flattop. Mr. R. and his student assistants put us through a rugged routine every gym day. Back then, I looked like the "98-pound weakling" in the Charles Atlas muscle-building courses advertised on the back pages of comic books. I had arms like wienies. The exercise I absolutely hated the most was climbing to the top of a wooden pole that hung down from the gym ceiling. The pole was about two inches in diameter and must have been twenty feet long. I never made it to the top like the more muscular guys did. Mr. Romeiser would stand at the bottom and watch us. When he could tell that one of us had gone as far as we could, he'd yell up, "Come on down, if that's the best you can do." It wasn't that he had any great compassion on us. I think he was half afraid that if he pushed me and my fellow wienies too hard, one of us might lose our grip and fall clear to the floor. And he might get fired over it.

The most fun thing we did in gym class was swing on a thick rope with a huge knot tied in the end. Like the wooden pole, the rope was attached to one of the trusses holding up the gym roof. We had to jump off a high horse, grab the rope as it swung towards us, swing across the width of the gym, and dismount by letting go and trying to land on our feet on a bunch of padded canvas mats. Of course, some of the clowns in class had to let out with a Tarzan-like yell while they were swinging. Most of us enjoyed taking an extra swing before letting go. We got by with it as long as Mr. Romeiser wasn't looking. If he caught anyone trying to pull anything they shouldn't, he'd make them do pushups as punishment. Maybe he was an ex-Marine drill sergeant. I don't know, but he sure looked and acted like one. When we started at the new school, my gym class was taught by Mr. Bridgeford. He was easier going than Mr. R. But, you know what? I actually missed that likable old grouch with his clipboard and whistle. He was a real character.

Industrial Arts had always been one of Manual's strongest areas of education. One of my favorite classes at old Manual was Wood Shop I. The antiquated shop was on the second floor at the far north end of the building. The place looked like a scene taken from a novel about the Industrial Revolution. All the machines had belt drives that went up to long shafts near the ceiling with large pulleys which turned the belts. With a bunch of rambunctious boys using the equipment, it was a miracle that none of us ever caught our hands in the thick leather belts. Fortunately, none of us ever did.

Our shop teacher was a little old guy named Mr. Mathers. He reminded me of Louie, the proprietor of the sweet shop in a popular series of comedy movies back then featuring Leo Gorcey and the Bowery Boys. Mr. Mathers was hard of hearing and didn't see too well either. He usually had on a shop apron and sometimes wore heavy black cloth protectors over his shirt sleeves. He favored bow ties for safety reasons because they wouldn't dangle down and get caught in running machinery like a regular long tie could.

The shop had several lathes for turning square pieces of wood into round objects. Several of the jokers among us (no, I was *not* one of them) thought they were being clever when they turned out giant phalluses. All the rest of us in the class had a good laugh when we realized what they were. Mr. Mathers didn't share our amusement. He made the culprits rework the shapes into something not obscene, like miniature baseball bats. If the truth were known, the making of giant replicas of male sex organs was probably something that had occurred at the beginning of many new semesters over his long years of teaching. As a result, Mr. Mathers was forewarned by experience to watch out for such antics and be prepared to apprehend the perpetrators.

Another unusual memory I have about wood shop was an occasional opportunity to take a quick peek at some of the girlie magazines that one of the boys smuggled in from time to time and passed around when the teacher wasn't looking. This was my first exposure to full-color photos of naked women. These were not the top-of-the-line nudie magazines that had high standards for the beauty of their naked models. Instead, they were low-class publications with names like *Bare Babes* and *Naughty Nudes*. They seemed to specialize in scuzzy women who looked like street walkers. But, despite their less-than-beautiful faces, these gals were willing to show *everything* they had. Such crude magazines served as our source of visual aids for learning about female anatomy in the absence of formal sex education classes. No wonder some of the guys were producing phallic images out of wood. They were probably horny from looking at those nasty pictures. We all felt like we were real men of the world after sharing such secretive material. Old Mr. Mathers was never any the wiser. If he was on the other side of the huge shop, we soon learned that he couldn't even see us across the room, let alone know what we were up to. When we eventually started classes down at the new Manual, Mr. Mathers was no longer around to apprehend any future phallus makers. He'd retired.

During my one semester at old Manual, I got stuck with the last lunch period of the day. I didn't eat until 12:45—or maybe it was 1:00 pm—and the selection of food available at such a late period didn't always include everything shown on that day's menu board. I remember one day going through the line trying to pick out something to eat from the meager leftovers presented. I came to the dessert section and spotted what I thought were several slices of cherry pie—one of my favorites. I had the lunch lady behind the counter plop a dip of vanilla ice cream on top. That would be my lunch for the day. Not exactly a well-balanced meal that Mom would approve of, but it was something I liked and would fill my growling stomach. I carried my tray over and sat as I usually did with Jim Barker, another freshman.

As I started eating the pie, I encountered strange hunks of slimy greenish stuff that looked like pieces of celery and tasted funny. I quickly decided that I didn't want the pie after all. Jim saw me spit it out. He chuckled and said, "What's the matter, Charlie. Don't you like *rhubarb* pie?" I'd never eaten rhubarb pie before in my life and this was not going to be the first time. In fact, it was the one-and-only time that rhubarb ever touched my lips. Yuck! I went ahead and ate the ice cream, but felt like I'd been ripped off and that they should have labeled what kind of pie it was for the benefit of unsuspecting people like me. I took the now-soggy pie up to the cashier and politely complained. But to no avail; that was the only kind of pie they had left (gee, I wonder why). All she could do was give me back my fifteen cents. I was happy, but still hungry.

With these few noteworthy exceptions, that's all I remember about the exciting and traumatic days of my first semester as a high school freshman. Funny what sticks in your mind through the years and what slips away. I'm sure there were many other fun and serious moments worth sharing. But they're lost somewhere in the forgetfulness that comes with the passing of time—and the aging of the brain that once stored them.

"Old" Manual as it looked when it was still new back in 1906 (built in 1895). View is looking toward southwest corner of building with Russell Avenue running past the front entrance and Merrill Street running along the south side.

24

Late Date

I was excited. It was a few minutes before nine on a Friday evening, the one night of the week Fisher's Market stayed open late. The store was nearly empty of customers and Mr. Fisher told me to go ahead and start sweeping the aisles. While pushing the broom around, I was already thinking about what I'd be doing after work. Don Stafford, a buddy of mine, and his girlfriend, Brenda, were picking me up when I got off. But that wasn't the only reason why I was so eager to finish up. The main reason was that Brenda had a girlfriend they were bringing along for me to meet. Sort of a blind double-date. That's what had me so excited as I finished up my sweeping.

I asked Mr. Fisher if he had anything else for me to do before I left. He said, "Did you already take out the trash?"

"Yes, sir." I replied. Through the window, I saw Don pull up to the curb out in front of the store. My eagerness to see what awaited me was growing by the minute.

"Okay. Then I guess that's all for tonight, Charlie." He added, "We'll see you tomorrow."

Mrs. Murphy, the store cashier, had already left. It was just me and the Fishers. I told them good night as he unlocked the front door and let me out. It had turned considerably colder than when I came to work at five. The air was biting as I hurried over to Don's 1950 Chevy. When I opened the door, everyone inside the car said "hi" as I climbed into the back seat. As I sat down next to the girl I'd never met before who was my date for the evening, I replied, "Hi, guys." She smiled at me.

My blind date turned out to be quite a gal. She had a little more meat on her bones than the average girl, but wasn't bad looking. Brenda introduced her to me as Janet Baker. We both said "hi" again, this time directly to each other. I didn't recognize Janet as anyone I'd seen at Manual High School where Don and I went. I asked her where she went to school; she said Sacred Heart. Hmmm. That meant she must be a Catholic. But I didn't hold that against her, even though I was a Protestant.

Janet had her coat off and piled up on the seat beside her. By the dim light of the dome lamp in Don's car, I could see that she was stacked – oh, was she ever. She had long brown hair and, shall we say, a somewhat prominent nose. Not too big, but almost. Any slight deficiencies she might have had in her looks, Janet more than made up for with her friendliness. We began talking like two old friends as Don pulled away. He said they'd already decided we'd head for the Tee Pee to get something to eat. That sounded good to me. I was really hungry—in more ways than one.

Janet's wadded-up coat was on her left side, so that put her right up against me on her right. I could feel warmth radiating out of her. No wonder she had her coat off. She was hot—literally. We headed across Sanders Street and hadn't even gotten to Shelby when Janet leaned over and whispered something in my ear. I loved it when a girl did that. The only problem was, she caught me off guard and I didn't understand what she said. So, I had to ask her in a near whisper, "What?"

She repeated in her soft voice, "Have you ever had a butterfly kiss?" I thought, *Oh, wow. We haven't gone four blocks and she's already asking me a question like that?* I'd never heard of a butterfly kiss, but any kind of a kiss was okay with me.

I whispered back to her, "No. I never have." I had to half bury my nose in her hair in order to whisper in her ear. It tickled, but I liked being that close to her. I don't know what shampoo she used, but her hair sure smelled good. Or maybe it was her perfume.

"Would you like one?" she asked as innocently as if she were offering me a stick of gum or a piece of candy. Now how do you think a red-blooded teenage boy is going to answer a girl who asks him a question like that? Of course, I said yes.

She reached up with her left hand, took hold of my chin, and gently tipped my head over closer to her face . As my left cheek neared her lips I was ready for whatever a butterfly kiss was. But no warm lips touched my awaiting cheek. Instead, I felt something lightly scratching it. Then, I realized she was fluttering her long eyelashes against my face. I guess she was supposed to be mimicking a butterfly fluttering its wings. Talk about being disappointed. What a letdown!

"So, that's what you call a butterfly kiss, huh?" I asked her. "I think I like the regular kind a lot better." By the passing streetlights I could see she was smiling. Then she laughed softly like the joke was on me. I felt like I'd been had. She must have sensed my disappointment because she leaned over and gave me a big wet kiss on the cheek. As she pulled back, she whispered, "So do I." Instantly, an alarm went off in my mind. I got the immediate impression that she was ready, willing, and able to start making out right then and there. Something told me this girl was "hot to trot," as boys used to say about girls who were overly eager to make out and maybe even to "go all the way." I'd only met Janet five minutes ago, for crying out loud. She was moving way too fast for me. Way too fast.

Since I didn't take the bait, Janet sat up straight and we all carried on a four-way conversation till we arrived at the Tee Pee. After pulling into a parking slot, we ordered and ate in the car. Don left the motor running and the heater cranked up, so we stayed warm enough. But the back windows still got steamed up, probably from the warmth exuded by Janet's hot body.

By the time we finished eating and talking, it was nearly ten-thirty. Don said, "I hate to be a party-pooper guys, but I gotta get up early tomorrow. We better call it a night." Don was a drummer in Manual's band and had to attend a special practice session the next morning. He headed for Janet's house to drop her off first. On our way there, among other things we talked about a certain movie showing uptown. We got the idea of going to see it on another double-date the following Sunday afternoon. Everyone agreed and we quickly made our plans. It was the easiest date I ever arranged.

Don pulled up in a parking area among some two-story brick apartment buildings. Janet said I didn't have to walk her up to the door. I said, "Okay, then. I'll see you Sunday." The dome light was on as she smiled at me and pursed her lips in a silent air-kiss. She climbed out of the back seat and said, "Bye, guys." Then, she threw her coat over her shoulders and ran toward one of the nearby buildings. I almost felt like running after her, but didn't. She definitely had me wanting more.

After Janet disappeared inside her front door and the porch light went off, Don backed out and we headed for my house. As we drove along, Brenda couldn't wait to ask me, "Well, how did you like Janet?" I knew I had to answer carefully because they were friends and I figured whatever I said she'd tell Janet.

So, I said, "She's quite a girl. Pretty cute and kind of a jokester." Then, I told them about Janet's butterfly kiss surprise. Brenda replied, "Oh, yeah. She likes to cut up a lot. And she sure has plenty of boyfriends." I didn't doubt it.

A few minutes later, Don stopped in front of my house and I climbed out. Before I closed the door, he said, "We'll pick you up around twelve-thirty on Sunday."

I said "Okay. See ya then." As I went up our walk and into the house, I was already thinking Sunday couldn't come soon enough. Even though she was a bit of an eager beaver, I'd enjoyed being with Janet—despite her catching me off guard with her little butterfly kiss trick. I looked forward to getting to know her better and maybe swapping some *real* kisses at the movie.

Sunday came and I wolfed down my lunch after church. I just had time to brush my teeth before Don was honking out in front. I told my folks good-by and headed out the door full of high hopes for my second date with Janet.

We drove down Shelby Street to the apartment project where Janet lived. Don pulled into the parking area, and I got out. Brenda pointed out the building Janet lived in (they all looked pretty much alike). The sun was shining brightly and I had a big grin of anticipation on my face as I walked up the steps to her front door. After ringing the bell, I stood there expecting Janet to answer the door. She didn't. No one did. I rang the bell again and waited what must have been a full minute. Still no answer. As I turned around to leave, I heard the door opening. I turned back hoping to see Janet's smiling face. Instead, a woman I assumed was her mother opened the storm door part way and said, "Yeah? What do you want?" She didn't look too happy to see me and I sure wasn't happy to see her sourpuss face.

I said, "I'm here to pick up Janet for our date to the movies."

Imagine my total surprise when the woman said with a sneer, "She can't go."

Stunned both by her look and her response, I stammered, "Uh, why not? Is she okay?" I expected her mother to say that Janet didn't feel well, or that something had come up in the family making it impossible for her to go. But she didn't.

As I stood there not believing what I was

hearing, the woman said, "Janet's grounded because she stayed out too late on a date Friday night."

I couldn't see her, but somewhere inside behind the scowling woman I heard a familiar voice say loudly, "MOM!" Her mother turned and looked away from the door as she half shouted over her shoulder, "You shut up. If you hadn't been out till two o'clock in the morning this wouldn't have happened."

Oh, boy! I didn't know what to say or what to do. I just stood there as the woman pulled the storm door shut in my face. I meekly said, "Okay." but I don't think the woman heard me.

I turned around and walked in a daze what seemed like a mile back to Don's car. I could see his and Brenda's puzzled faces as I approached. After I got in, they asked me what was going on. I told them the whole episode briefly and that Janet *wasn't* coming with us. Even though she was Janet's friend, I could tell Brenda was really upset about the situation. But she couldn't have been any madder than I was. They both felt sorry for me and Don said, "You can still come with us and go to the movie." It was a nice gesture, but somehow it didn't sound like something I wanted to do. I didn't want to be a spare tire on their date, so I said, "No, I don't think so. Thanks, anyway. Just drop me off at my house and you two go on." It was a mighty quiet ride back to Wright Street. Nobody knew what to say, so none of us said much of anything.

When we arrived at my house, I told them to have a good time and thanks, again. By then, I was on the verge of crying, but didn't want to in front of them. So, I waved good-bye and hurried inside. My folks were naturally surprised to see me back so soon and asked me what was wrong. I gave them a quick version of what happened while I struggled to keep control, then headed up to my room.

After changing clothes, I flopped on my bed. As I lay there staring at the ceiling and thinking over what'd happened, tears welled up in my eyes and ran down both sides of my face. It made me mad that Janet couldn't go to the movies with me because of what she'd done with another boy. Plus, she'd really embarrassed me in front of my friends. And what *really* burned me up was the fact that she'd gone out with another guy on Friday night *after* her date with me—and stayed out till *two* in the morning? What kind of a wild woman was she? I wasn't so sure I wanted to date a girl like that after all. But the sting of what she'd done still hurt me deeply in a way I'd never been hurt before.

I lay there wondering if she'd pulled her butterfly kiss trick on whoever the other guy was on her late date. Somehow, I imagined that it went way, way beyond butterflies. And I discovered for the first time in my young life that a girl can break a boy's heart.

I never saw Janet again.

25

Onward, Manual!

After completing my first semester of high school at the "old" Manual, the new facility opened in the fall of 1953—even though it wasn't quite finished. The building was completed and the utilities were functioning, but the campus landscaping hadn't even been started. The lockers weren't installed, the cafeteria wasn't equipped to serve meals yet, and lots of other minor details were still being worked on. So, the student body was alphabetically divided into two groups, each going half a day to shortened classes. We had to carry our coats, books, and anything else we needed around with us since we had no lockers. This lasted for several weeks and we quickly got used to it—many students liked it that way, despite the inconveniences involved. When we finally received our lockers and began the regular all-day schedule, it seemed like we were in classes for endless hours each school day.

Our new lockers were installed in the walls of the hallways and had built-in combination locks instead of padlocks. I was always afraid I'd forget my combination, so kept it written on a card in my wallet. One day I forgot to carry my wallet. And wouldn't you know that was the same day I also couldn't remember my locker combination. As a result, I had to go to the school office and confess my memory lapse, plus my failure to be prepared by having the numbers written down somewhere. The short lecture I received from the less-than-understanding lady in the office—who was probably bothered by numerous other forgetful students on a regular basis—was sufficient to ensure that I never, ever let this happen again. Believe it or not, I still after all these years have an occasional nightmare about this incident. Don't ask me why, but it must have traumatized me even more than I thought at the time.

While in my second semester as a freshman, I still had my paper route, so rode my bike to and from school each day. The distance was further to the new Manual than it had been to the old—about two miles instead of only one. The new facility had outdoor bike racks in the middle of a small parking area behind the auto shop. One day after school, I went out and unlocked my bike. As I was wiping beads of water off the seat from a rain shower that had occurred earlier, I noticed a couple of guys I didn't know watching me as they stood in the open overhead doorway of the auto shop. After drying off the seat the best I could using my handkerchief, I jumped on my bike and started to peddle away. As I did, one of the smart aleck auto shop students yelled out, "Oooh, look at the little boy riding his bicycle." I made no reply to this thoughtless insult, but rode away as quickly as possible while they stood there laughing. That was the *last* day I ever bicycled to high school. From then on, I rode the city bus. I was approaching fifteen and my bicycling days were over.

Of all the classes I took at Manual, the one that turned out to be the most useful throughout my later life was typing. Yes, I actually wanted to learn how to use a typewriter (computers were still decades in the future). The fact that the typing classes were comprised entirely of girls may have been an added incentive, but that *wasn't* my primary reason—it really wasn't.

The first day I walked into my typing classroom it was already filled wall-to-wall with girls. The smell of estrogen was so strong I could almost taste it. Or maybe it was just the overpowering scent of fourteen different perfumes that made my tongue tingle. Anyway, it was an odd combination of my best dream (being surrounded by dozens of girls) and my worst nightmare (trying to look and act cool around dozens of girls).

The teacher sympathized with me and reminded all the young ladies not to tease me for being the only boy in the class. She also made me feel better by saying that she thought more boys should take typing. That statement brought forth an approving buzz from the girls that made me feel like I'd be accepted. As it turned out, I was.

A couple of girls even took me under their wings and helped me out when I had questions or problems and didn't want to ask the teacher. One was Bev Wells, who sat next to me, and her friend Carol Rice, who sat near us in the alphabetized seating arrangement. I thought Carol was really cute and eventually mentioned it to Bev. Naturally, she relayed my feelings to Carol, but I didn't mind. In fact, I figured she would. I was just on the verge of asking Carol out when Cupid shot me with an arrow bearing someone else's name: Joyce Van Lue. After meeting Joyce, I only had eyes for her from then on and Carol became the road not taken. Who knows? My life story might have been completely changed if the timing of things had been a little different.

I ended up taking both Typing I and II and became quite proficient, although I always had trouble typing numbers—and still do. One of my first major purchases with money I'd stashed away in my savings account was a Royal portable typewriter with pica-size type. It served me well through college and for years afterward. Later in life, when I transitioned to using a computer, I was really glad I'd taken typing back in high school.

Even though I grew up with absolutely zero musical abilities and no other entertainment talents, I always enjoyed attending the plays, talent shows, operettas, concerts, and the annual Redskin Revue at Manual. This show was the biggest entertainment event of the school year and consisted of productions written, directed, and staged entirely by students. Each production was a combination of popular songs of the day, as well as some old standards, which were woven into a story of some kind loosely based on a movie or a Broadway show. Various acts were included featuring tap dancers, ballerinas, baton twirlers, singers, and any other talented students who could possibly be worked into the story. Weeks and weeks of preparation, costume and scenery making, and rehearsals went into these shows.

The Revue was presented on a Friday and Saturday night. Nicely printed programs were passed out by cute girls in formals serving as usherettes. On Saturday, at the conclusion of the show, the principal announced which production had been named the overall winner, as well as who was chosen as best male performer and best female performer. Much-coveted trophies were presented to the winners. After the awards ceremony, the kids from each of the acts held cast parties, whether they'd won or not.

Manual had its own weekly newspaper,

The Booster, which was published every Friday. A dedicated group of students worked hard to put these issues together and filled them with photos, stories, and ads for things of interest to our students. Many of these writers and photographers also worked on putting together and publishing the annual school yearbook, *The Ivian*. Newer students probably wondered why the yearbook had such a weird name. It was named after the ivy that grew on the walls of the old building that Manual had occupied for decades before moving to the new facility. Since I was a student in the very last class fortunate enough to attend school in the old building for a semester before moving to the new one, I knew this little bit of school history.

Other Manual memories include the dances: freshman mixers, after-game sock hops, the winter Snow Whirl, the Cherry Tree Hop, and the Junior and Senior proms. I never was much of a dancer, but attended most of these just to be there with my friends. In addition to these fun social times, there were several more serious scholastic and service-related organizations at Manual. These included: League of Honor, Roines (for senior boys) and Masoma (for senior girls), National Honor Society, Senior Council, and the Student Affairs Board.

If a student couldn't find a team, club, or other special interest group to join, it wasn't because of a lack of opportunity. There were sports teams including wrestling, baseball, golf, archery, basketball, football, track, and cross country, plus intramural sports. In addition to sports, Manual offered Mask & Wig, National Thespians, Stage Crew, Ham Radio Club, Quill & Scroll, News Bureau, Aero Weather Club, Camera Club, Wig-Wam Workers, Band, Band Color Guard, Pep Band, Pep Club, Dance Band, German Band, Orchestra, Lettermen's Club, FHA Club, FNA Club, FTA Club, Junior Red Cross, Tri-Hi-Y, Cub Club, Girls State, Boys State, ROTC Officer's Club, ROTC Drill Team, ROTC History Club, ROTC Rifle Team, ROTC Sponsors, Girl's Glee Club, Radio Speech Club, Model U.N., Y Teens Club, Dotty & Dan Bean Supper (an annual fund raiser), Senior Choir, Manualaires, Swords Club, Business Girls Club, Spanish Club, I. U. Journalism Institute, Baton Twirlers, Flag Girls, Cheerleaders, Record Club, Music Memory Contest, Essay Contest, Spring Pow Wow, Quiz 'Em Team, Glee-ettes, Top Ten, Lo-Per-Man Contest, Ensemble, Twirling Club, Cadet Teachers, Science Fair, and Girl's Bowling League. If I've forgotten any, it wasn't on purpose. How on earth did we have time to do our schoolwork with all these activities and meetings going on? I don't know but, somehow, we managed. And we had lots of fun and made lifelong friends while we did.

During the years I spent at Manual, I somehow managed to avoid a number of classes and activities that most every student was in at least one of. These included ROTC, foreign language classes (neither Spanish nor Latin), any kind of music class or related singing or playing group, and sports. I had absolutely no musical ability, nor was I an athlete. My class schedule was heavy in art, industrial arts, math, science, and history. I probably was what later became known as a nerd. Back then, we were thought of, if not called, bookworms or brains. I guess these were meant as insults, but we took them as compliments.

I volunteered during my free periods during several semesters to serve as a hall monitor. These monitors were boys and girls who each sat at small desks located along the hallways at all the stairway and exit doors. Our sworn duty was to challenge any students seen in the halls after classes started to make sure they weren't sneaking out of the building. If they didn't have a pass, we were supposed to report them to the office by requiring them to sign their name and the time they were apprehended in a logbook we each kept. I don't think this system worked too well because, if a monitor didn't personally know or recognize the offender, any name could be written in the book and we wouldn't know if it was correct or not. We usually never saw anyone in the halls and used the hour to study or goof-off a little. Sometimes my buddy, Mo Profeta, who was a monitor on the floor above me, would sneak down the stairs and we'd shoot the breeze for a while. We thought we were really getting away with something.

Kids were generally well-behaved in those days. Chewing gum in class was about the worst offense committed. Some teachers would order you to spit it out; others would tell you to swallow it. This could easily be faked and the gum hidden under your tongue so you could begin chewing it again later. Smoking was practically unheard of in high school and the few (mostly boys) who did would usually sneak out behind the auto shop building to indulge their forbidden habit. Others would occasionally "puff a weed " in a toilet stall. They were hidden from view, but the smoke cloud hovering over them betrayed what they were up to. If caught, offenders were taken to the school office, their parents notified, and a suspension given. Yes, just for smoking.

Fights in school were rare, but were always a source of great excitement when they did occur. If they were spontaneous, the result might be a shoving match in the hall. If they were more serious, they were of the "meet me out in the parking lot after school and we'll settle this later" type. In a few cases I heard about, but never personally witnessed, boys wanting to fight were taken to the school gym, made to put on boxing gloves, and told to duke it out. Afterward, they were required to shake hands and that was that. There were cliques and social clubs in those days, but no organized gangs. So personal grudges didn't escalate into warfare. A few of the really "tough" guys might have had a switchblade knife in their pocket or sock, but it was more to show off with than to cut anybody. The only guns on campus were the rifles used by the boys in ROTC. There were no resident policemen, no metal detectors, no drug-sniffing dogs, no special counselors. None of these were needed in those innocent times.

Not many girls got pregnant during my high school years at Manual. For the few who did, it was considered a major social shame to get "knocked up" (as it was called by other kids) and such girls had to quit school. As a result, they served as an example of what *not* to do. Strict standards of moral behavior were enforced back then. A boy couldn't even walk down the school hall holding hands or with his arm around his girl friend. I found this out the hard way one day when I was a senior and going steady with Joyce Van Lue, my high school sweetheart. I was proudly walking her down the hallway to her home economics class one day with my arm around her shoulders . Suddenly, someone grabbed my arm and yanked it away. I was ready to punch the person responsible until I turned around and saw that it was the Dean of Girls. I hadn't noticed her standing in a doorway as we passed. She was quick to say, "Young man, we don't behave like that here at Manual." Embarrassed in front of my true love, I mumbled a quick apology and we went on down the hallway. As soon as we got out of the dean's sight around the bend in the hall, my arm went right back where it had been around Joyce's shoulders. I felt like a real rebel.

I went to Manual an extra semester from January until June. I loved high school and was in no hurry to get out—especially since I was going steady with Joyce. My schedule was light that last semester, so I was able to work at a part-time job as a draftsman for a civil engineering and surveying company with offices uptown. I could catch an Indianapolis Transit System bus right in front of the school and ride it to within a block or two of my job. I also worked there on Saturdays. It was good experience and allowed me to earn decent money while still in school.

Not every teenage boy in my day owned a car; I was among those who didn't. Believe it or not, I somehow managed to carry on an active social life without one (even though borrowing the family car was never an option). Love finds a way. And I found mine. When I began dating Joyce, I knew she loved me for being me, not because of my car—because I didn't even own one.

From the details of the current situation given in a series of articles in *The Indianapolis*

Star, Manual High School is doomed due to a combination of changing demographics, lower scholastic expectations, lack of school spirit, failure to attend classes, rampant pregnancies, and the pervasive influence of drugs. What a sad ending it will be for such a once-great high school that decades of graduates still remember with great fondness. If the dire prophecy of doom does come true, who's to blame? Parents? Teachers? The students? School administrators? Deteriorating morals and weakened mores in our society? "All of the above" may be the correct answer to this difficult question.

Kids back in the "Golden Decade" of the 1950s weren't perfect. But nearly all of us went to school every day, did our homework most of the time, participated in extra-curricular activities, caused no trouble, were proud of our school, and worked hard to graduate and make something of ourselves. Yes, we were PROUD of Manual, its heritage, its accomplishments, its future promise. If the Manualites of today could go back and see what their high school was like in its glory days, they might be inspired and motivated toward greater achievements—but I wouldn't count on it. Maybe, like the doomsayers predict, it's already too late for Manual. Far too late.

Someday, maybe sooner than we think, a great high school will have suffered and finally died as the result of a long process that began forty-five years ago with the gutting of a once-thriving neighborhood, including several blocks of Wright Street where I grew up. And it was all done in the name of progress when the interstate highways were built through Indianapolis. In retrospect, it seems like what's happening to Manual and the surrounding area is much, much too high a price to pay just for the ability to move traffic at higher speeds across the south side of our city. Too high a price indeed.

So, good-bye Manual. It was great knowing you and a privilege being a part of you. Our fond memories of you live on and are treasured in the hearts and minds of we who once walked your halls, sat in your classrooms, went to your games, participated in your activities, and were filled with pride when, together, we sang:

Onward, Manual, on forever,
Always to success.
Let your banner never waver,
Failure ne'er confess. (Rah! Rah! Rah!)

Onward, Manual, ever onward,
Make a glorious name.
Strive upward, strive and gain
An envied fame.

Manual High School, Class of 1957,
Roines - Senior Boys' Honorary Organization.
FRONT ROW: Kent Klinge, Rudy Gayde, me, Paul Schnepf. SECOND ROW: Mr. Richard Blough (sponsor), Don Kerner, Maurice Bush, Bill Bruhn, and Howard Smiley. THIRD ROW: Daniel Chapell, Jerry Adams, Gary Beplay, Don Weddle, and Gordon Harnack. BACK ROW: David Kriech, Tom McCormick, Kenny Bryant, Brice Tressler, and Gerald DeHoney.

26

The Vanishing of Jack Wesley

One semester at the new Manual, my English teacher was the infamous Mr. John Moffat. He was a short, elderly man with white hair and a twisted sense of humor. Every day, he wore the same blue suit, white shirt, and red tie, or maybe he had several of each. His main method of teaching was to use sarcasm and take bold action that made a lasting impression on his students. His reputation was such that some kids prayed they would never be assigned to him for English class. I was different; I actually looked forward to it.

Among Mr. Moffat's favorite tricks was, when noting spelling and punctuation errors in an essay assignment he was grading, to take his pencil and punch a hole through the page where each error occurred. Then, when returning the papers to the students, he'd come to one with a hole (or holes) in it and say, "Oh, my. Here's one with a big hole in it. I can't accept that. Take it and do it over." Then, he would throw the paper on the floor in front of his desk and the unlucky student he'd named had to come forward and retrieve it. Once you experienced this, you were more careful to spell words correctly and use proper punctuation next time. I learned my lesson after only one such experience. Others were doomed to be repeaters.

Mr. Moffat kept a thick cushion on the old-fashioned, wooden desk chair in his classroom. We never knew the reason for the cushion, whether it was to boost him up so he could see better or if he had a tender butt. One day Jack Wesley entered the classroom a few minutes early and saw that our teacher wasn't there yet. Jack quickly grabbed the cushion off the chair and hid it in the closet before Mr. Moffat arrived. When he came in and started to sit down, he immediately noticed his cushion was missing. There were several stifled snickers among us; Mr. Moffat, however, was *not* in the least amused.

Mr. Moffat asked the class who the culprit was. Nobody said a word. He asked again. Still no reply. We could tell that he was getting really steamed up about it because his usual pink face was turning red. Finally, he said, "Alright, *children,* then we'll just sit here until the thief who took my cushion decides to confess and returns it to my chair. And if nobody does, then you'll *all* get an F for the day." After several minutes of awkward silence, Jack finally raised his hand and confessed his misdeed.

Mr. Moffat asked him where the cushion

was. Jack went to the closet, retrieved the missing cushion, handed it over, and started to return to his seat. Mr. Moffat looked at the cushion and was even more upset when he discovered that one of the ties had been broken when Jack yanked the cushion off the chair. Mr. Moffat said in a stern voice, "Oh, no you don't. Don't go to your seat Mr. Wesley, go stand in the closet for the rest of the period." Jack turned around and looked at Mr. Moffat as though he were kidding, but he wasn't—he was dead serious. So, Jack went over and entered the closet, but left the door open. Mr. Moffat said, "Close the door, please. I don't want to see your face looking at me. And think about what you did while you're in there." Jack meekly closed the door and the rest of us finally got started on the day's lesson.

At the end of the class period, as we all got up to leave the room, Mr. Moffat went over to the closet and opened the door. As it swung open he said, "You can come out now and I hope you've learned a lesson from this, Mr. Wesley." But guess what? When the door was fully open it revealed that the closet was *empty*! Jaws dropped in amazement and some of the girls gasped. All of us were mystified about Jack's unexpected disappearance—and Mr. Moffat most of all. He was obviously puzzled as he stood there scratching the thatch of white hair on top of his head and asked we who had gathered around, "Wha . . . Where on earth did he go?" None of us had a clue. It was like Jack had literally vanished into thin air.

We all had to get to our next class and the room quickly cleared out. Mr. Moffat was left behind still looking into the closet as if he expected Jack to suddenly reappear. Some of us ran into Jack down the hallway and he quickly explained—somewhat triumphantly—how he'd pulled off his disappearing act. He told us there was space above the ceiling tiles for the ductwork, wiring, and plumbing. The closets had no ceiling tiles in them and Jack had managed to climb up into the utility space, very carefully and quietly crawl across the top side of the ceiling while holding on to a large pipe, and then come down in the closet of the empty classroom next door to the one we had English in. We all had a good laugh about it and complimented Jack on his cleverness and agility. His trick was buzzed about all over school for a day or two. I don't know if Mr. Moffat ever figured out how Jack pulled it off.

The vanishing of Jack Wesley from the closet may have been the only time that a student ever put one over on Mr. Moffat. If so, it deserves to go into the record book. Unfortunately, there is no record book for such dubious, but memorable, achievements. So, telling about the incident in *this* book will have to do.

Good one, Jack!

Like all the other stories in this book, this one is absolutely true. The only thing I made up was the name "Jack Wesley." I wracked my brain trying to think of who the guy was who pulled this disappearing trick. No luck. If you remember who he was, let me know and I'll give him proper credit in future editions.

27

The Absolutely Incredible Long Shot

I'll admit it. I was never much of an athlete while growing up. Whenever sides were chosen for any kind of team in grade school gym class or in a neighborhood pick-up game, I was usually the *last* choice. You know, the one who made the other kids already chosen groan or roll their eyes when they saw that I would be on their team. So, sports just never had much attraction for me. As a teenager, however, I developed a great interest in attending my high school's football and basketball games. Why? The answer was simple: I wanted to be with my buddies and we wanted to see girls. And the girls we wanted to see were at the Friday night ballgames. If the truth were known, this was the main reason most of the guys attended. And if our team beat the other team, well that was just icing on the cake. But the cake was being around the girls.

Even though I was no sports aficionado, one Manual High School basketball game during my junior year still stands out in my mind.

It was the night Pat Clancy made his what-would-become-famous, game-winning long shot. Pat was my age and lived in the Fountain Square neighborhood; his house was over on Leonard Street, a block east of me, between Prospect and Woodlawn. With a good Irish name like Clancy, Pat may have been a Catholic. If he was, he could have gone to Cathedral or Sacred Heart, or maybe to Scecina. But he didn't, he went to good old Manual. And on that night we were especially fortunate that Pat was a Redskin wearing number 21.

The unforgettable night of Pat's triumph was a home game; Manual was playing our arch rival, Tech. It had been a close-fought contest with the lead alternating back-and-forth several times. Late in the fourth quarter, Tech was leading by two. But the score was tied 50-50 after Pat hit a great one-hander from near mid-court. Then, with the last seconds ticking away, Tech had possession and came charging toward their end of the court. Pat darted in and stole the ball. I remember it clearly because my best buddy, Dick Foster, and I were down at floor level getting a head start for the exit. We thought sure Tech would make one final basket and beat Manual again, as they had every year for over two decades—oh, we of little faith. I was watching the action from the sideline, right at the edge of the court and as close to Pat as any spectator could be.

Just as the clock ran out and the horn blew, Pat made a last-second desperation shot. He bent low and with all his might let go with a tremendous two-handed push shot while he was still close to Tech's keyhole. After the ball left his hands, he stood there frozen for an instant while the ball arced high over nearly the full length of the court. A thousand pairs of eyes on each side of the court followed the ball in its flight as everyone held their breath. Those who were still seated leapt to their feet and joined those already standing. The crowd was instantly silent; only the continuing sound of the buzzer was heard. As the ball started its descent, the hushed crowd eagerly anticipated whether it would hit or miss the target. The odds, of course, greatly favored a miss. But, then . . . SWISH! The ball dropped perfectly through the hoop without even touching the backboard—Pat nailed it and made that absolutely incredible, once-in-a-lifetime, two-pointer. Final score: Manual 52, Tech 50. The game was over and Manual—thanks to Pat—had beaten Tech for the first time in twenty-five years!

For a few seconds, I don't think Pat could believe that he'd actually made such an impossible shot as he stood there rubbing his eyes and shaking his head. There may have been a tear or two, but if so they were hidden by the sweat on his face. Then, the crowd literally went wild. All of us on Manual's side started jumping up and down, slapping one another on the back, and screaming like we were crazy. People who didn't even know one another began hugging like old friends. Several guys—including me—whistled loudly to cheer the victory. Others, still up on the wooden pull-out bleachers, began stomping their feet in rhythm and added to the pandemonium. Some of the girls were so emotional they started crying. Several younger adults who had never ever seen a Manual victory over Tech shed a few tears, too.

Pat's teammates, including those from the bench, all rushed over and mobbed him, leaping and bouncing as they came running across the floor. They lifted Pat up on their shoulders and began parading him around the court like the hero he was. Pat always had a great smile, but I'd never seen him grin as widely as he did that night. His jaw muscles must have been sore the next day. Another guy wearing a big grin was Coach Cummins. Sure, it was a real squeaker; but a win was a win, and he was obviously plenty happy about it.

The pep band immediately began blasting out our school song. They played "Onward, Manual" over and over and over again. I thought the bass drummer was going to bust the heads on his drum. Some Manualites sang along, while others kept up the roar. A few couples actually started dancing in the aisle along the front of Manual's bleachers. The combined noise of all the shouting, clapping, whistling, stomping, loud music, and singing was nearly deafening as it bounced off the gym's concrete block walls. The crowd kept the euphoria going like they never wanted it to stop. And we didn't. Twenty-five years of disappointment and frustration were erased that night in twenty-five minutes of continuous celebration.

As you can imagine, Tech's fans just stood there in shock. Some were shaking their heads in disbelief. Their cheerleaders were all crying and huddled together trying to comfort one another. Even though Tech lost, their team honored such a truly remarkable accomplishment. As most of the Greenclad players snapped out of their shock, they showed their good sportsmanship by offering congratulations to Pat and his teammates with lots of back slapping and hand shaking.

I wouldn't have believed what Pat did if I hadn't been there and witnessed it with my own eyes. Yeah, it no doubt took luck to make a basket from such a distance. Many people consider seven a so-called lucky number, and Pat's 21 was *three times seven*. So, who knows? Maybe he was triple-blessed with the so-called "luck of the Irish" that memorable night in Manual's gymnasium. But skill had something to do with it too. Remember, just half a minute earlier, Pat had sunk a basket shooting from mid-court to tie the game.

Pat's game-winning basket went into the Manual record books and became part of south side history. It grew into a legend that people still talk about today. Though I never played any sports in high school, it was obvious even to me that this was one of those rare and unforgettable moments of true athletic greatness. And I was privileged to be there and see it the night Pat Clancy made his absolutely incredible long shot.

Way to go, Pat!

After graduating from Manual, Pat followed a career path that eventually led to his becoming an international diamond merchant. After years of success and frequent travel to the diamond and gemstone capitals of the world, he retired in 1992 to pursue other business and personal interests. Pat currently resides in northwestern Hancock County.

28

G-strings and Pasties

CAUTION: The following story is rated "R" because it contains material that may be considered offensive by some readers. Most of you, however, will probably find it quite amusing. READ AT YOUR OWN RISK.

Every major city has its seamy side, and Indianapolis in the 1950s was no exception. In addition to a rumored downtown "red light" district (I was never quite sure exactly where this was) and plenty of sleazy bars and other night spots, there were a few movie theaters like the Esquire which showed racy "adults-only" films. If you didn't know them by reputation, you could usually tell which theaters fell into this category by their lurid advertisements in the theater section of the newspaper. Respectable citizens tolerated these various dives, but wouldn't be caught dead in any of them. There were a few exceptions, however, and Dick Foster (my best buddy) and I were two of them.

One night during the summer of my senior year in high school, we dared to venture into the very center of hard-core wickedness in downtown Indianapolis: the Fox Theater. This was one of the few burlesque theaters in the Midwest that still had their doors open. There had once been a second burlesque theater downtown, the Mutual. But it had gone out of business a couple of years before we were old enough (or, in my case, *almost* old enough) to go. Burlesque was originally a legitimate art form, but over the decades had deteriorated into a crude combination of raunchy strippers and vulgar comedians—most of which were well past their prime. In fact, burlesque itself was in its twilight years as an entertainment genre. But the Fox ads in the newspaper, plus its sinister reputation whispered among older teenage boys, reached out with its siren song of temptation. And we couldn't resist the call. We wanted to see live women take off their clothes and the Fox was the place to see them do it.

We drove uptown in Dick's old Chevy on a week night, avoiding the weekend on purpose because we figured the Fox would be more crowded then. After parking on a dark side street (so no adult who knew Dick would see his car and tell his parents where they'd seen it), we walked around the corner to the brightly lit front of the Fox. We'd heard there was an age limit of eighteen for admission. I think Dick was close to that and looked a little older than he was. I, on the other hand, thought I looked more like thirteen or fourteen than my actual seventeen-and-a-half. And with my never-been-shaved cheeks and short flattop haircut, I looked like the obvious teenager that I was. I was nervous and afraid the ticket seller in the booth out front would ask me to prove my age. But, as it turned out, I needn't have worried.

Dick bought his ticket first with no problems. He stepped aside and it was my turn. My insides were doing flip-flops as I plunked down my two dollars and fifty cents and held my breath. The theater was on hard times and the ticket man was not about to turn anyone away. He just tore one off the roll and slid it over to me without even looking up. Somehow, I don't think he would've challenged me even if he'd taken a good look at my youthful face speckled with teenage acne.

Greatly relieved and almost giddy with excitement we entered into the jaws of the beast. We didn't tarry outside looking at any of the giant posters of the featured headliners. We were afraid someone who knew us might drive by on Illinois Street and spot us. A telltale phone call to our parents would have landed us—me anyway—in big trouble. I could just imagine my parents grilling me and asking, "What on earth were you doing in a place like THAT? Didn't we raise you better? Oh, where did we fail?" I guess maybe that was my conscience talking to me. But in vain. Lucky for us we got inside before being spotted by any well-meaning tattlers. My next fear was that I would run into some adult *inside* the theater who might know me. Again, it was a needless concern.

Hardly anyone was in the lobby, and what few there were looked like derelicts. Some of them eyed Dick and me a little funny, like we didn't belong there—or maybe it was my imagination. We decided we'd better go to the restroom before finding seats. We quickly spotted the men's room sign which pointed down a wide stairway to the basement. I was glad there were two of, so we could watch out for each other. We both kept our eyes open and looking all around as if expecting some dirty old pervert to jump out of a stall and flash his privates at us. Again, we had no need to worry because we were the only ones in the restroom. As I remember, it was pretty grungy and the kind of place where you didn't even want to touch the faucets, let alone flush the toilet. We were glad to get out of that stinking hole and head back upstairs to more breathable air.

The show hadn't started yet and the house lights were still turned on. They were way brighter than I expected and I was again afraid that someone in the theater might recognize me. We wanted to sit close enough to the stage to be able to see "everything," but not so close as to be out in front of everyone else. We slid into a couple of seats about six rows from the stage and hunkered down. Looking around, I could see no more than a couple dozen people in the whole place. They were scattered here and there in ones and twos—mostly guys by themselves. One of the men had a woman with him. I thought this sure seemed like a crummy place to bring a date. I wondered if the woman was as scared as I was. There were a few box seats set high up in the side walls near each end of the stage. A couple of them held loners. I noticed that one of the guys was wearing a raincoat (more about him later).

Before they would start the evening's revue, we had to sit through what had evidently become a pre-show routine in burlesque's later years. A couple of old guys shuffled down the two main aisles and stood in front of the audience with carriers full of boxes of something. Another guy, maybe the owner or manager, started giving a hard sales pitch about this wonderful caramel corn, or candy, or maybe it was fudge. Whatever it was, it was "only" a dollar—but that was nearly half the price we'd paid for admission. The man assured everyone that it was well worth the price because each box contained a naughty prize guaranteed to delight the buyer—the pitchman almost made it sound like X-rated Cracker Jack.

Among the various prizes promised was a little plastic viewer showing a picture of a beautiful woman that when held up to a light bulb would show her absolutely naked. Neither Dick nor I wanted one bad enough to eat anything touched by the hands of people who worked in a place like this. So, we resisted the offer, but a few suckers in the audience took the bait. From what I could tell, none of them received the highly desired naked woman viewers. It looked like all they got were cheap "eight-page bibles" instead. After prolonging this routine until it became obvious that no one else was going to buy anything, the pitchman said the show would now begin. At last!

The house lights dimmed slowly and a trio of musicians in the orchestra pit eventually began belting out an opening song, followed by a big fanfare. The music was supplied by a piano player, a trumpeter (who doubled on sax, trombone, and clarinet), and, of course, the requisite drummer. They put out a lot of music that wasn't really that bad. These guys were probably all professionals whose musical careers had ended in the pit at the Fox. What a waste of good talent.

The glory days of burlesque were long past. We soon discovered that there was no lavish scenery and no chorus lines of beautiful babes in revealing costumes with giant feathered headdresses. There was none of the stuff we expected to see from what was portrayed in old movies. It turned out to be just a plain stage with one stripper (or, *striptease artiste* as they preferred to be called) at a time going through her routine. And the act was nearly the same in every case. About the only thing that varied was the girls' hair color and the color of their costumes. But, when you've never seen real, live women taking their clothes off before, it was still fascinating stuff for a couple of hot-blooded teenage boys.

The first dish on the menu was a tall redhead named Dixie Belle. I wouldn't say she was overweight, but she was certainly well nourished. Right away she ran into trouble. They didn't have Velcro in those days and Dixie couldn't get the zipper on the back of her dress undone. She bravely tried to keep up the appearance that nothing was wrong as she struggled with it. Out of desperation, she danced over to the side curtain where we could see a guy yanking on the zipper until it finally came down. All the while she kept smiling and weaving to the music—and we kept snickering. After peeling her way through numerous layers of clothing, she was down to a fringed bra and skimpy panties covered with sequins. Her pale white skin was unblemished from head to toe except for a bruise (or maybe it was a birthmark?) on her thigh. But it hardly detracted from the totality of her near nakedness. My eyes were focused on her every move for fear of missing something. I hardly blinked.

Dick and I noticed that as she got closer

and closer to being naked (or as near to it as she legally could) the filter color on the spotlight up in the balcony that followed her every bump and grind grew darker and darker. When she first came out, it was a pure white spot. After her heavily brocaded evening gown finally came off, the light turned pale blue. After her bustier came off, the light went to dark blue. By the time she got down to her G-string and pasties, the light was dark magenta and we could barely see her (pardon the pun).

As her number ended, Dixie surprised everyone by yanking off her pasties. It was so dark on the stage by then that we couldn't really see much. I think she had on a smaller pair of pasties under the large ones she removed. I almost wished she hadn't done it because I was afraid there might be an undercover cop in the audience who would go call for a vice raid on the theater. Such things had happened in the past in some cities, but not very often, and never in Indianapolis. Not yet anyway. I was thinking it would be just my dumb luck for the vice squad to raid the Fox the one time I was there. I could just imagine reporters and photographers outside eagerly snapping pictures of the lewd entertainers being led off to the paddy wagon for corrupting the public morals while their lascivious fans—including Dick and me—looked on or covered our faces in shame.

Dixie's strip act was immediately followed by another one pretty much like it. Same routine, different girl. We noticed that when each stripper took off an item of clothing, she wouldn't just drop it on the floor. She'd dance her way over to the side curtain and hand the item to a man whose arm could be seen reaching out to receive it. The floor of the stage was probably so filthy that the dancers didn't want to dirty their costumes.

After our second dose of indecent exposure, the announcer told us we were in for a special treat because they had not one, but two, comedians who were now going to entertain us. They turned out to look an awful lot like the two guys who'd been trying to sell the X-rated boxes of fudge earlier. I'll never forget their names: one was Scurvy Ray Knob and the other was Sammy Spears. They came on stage and began talking back and forth and taking turns at being the straight man for each other. As they worked their way through a series of dirty jokes, the drummer provided a well-timed rim shot after each punch line as if to cue the audience when they were *supposed* to laugh. But not many did. I sensed that the unamused audience members just wanted to get this time-killing part over with and get back to what they'd really come to see: the strippers.

Scurvy and Sammy's routine was probably as old as the hills. But Dick and I'd never heard it before and laughed more than anyone else there. We tried to stifle our amusement so as not to draw attention to ourselves as obvious burlesque show novices. I still remember one bit they did. Scurvy was supposed to be a headline writer applying for a job at a newspaper. Sammy told him, "Okay. I'll give you a little test to see how well you can make up a headline for a news event using as few words as possible. Let's say a crazy guy escapes from a mental institution and rapes a woman. How would you word the headline?" Scurvy scratched his head as if deep in thought, then said, "I've got it. How about this? NUT BOLTS AND SCREWS!" The rest of the audience just emitted an audible groan, but Dick and I could hardly suppress our laughter. After a few more such groaners, the two comics ended their routine and we got back to the skin show.

The next gal was a buxom blonde aptly named Busty Taylor. She went through her act to the sensuous beat of "Shangri-La" all the while chewing gum and wearing the same bored look that the last girl had. Her mouth may have worn a smile, but you could tell in her eyes that she had done this so many times before that she was only going through the motions. Busty did have a novelty feature in her act. It was sort of a fancy bed, that stood about three feet high and was tilted upward from the foot. After taking off her dress and the next piece or two of her multilayered costume and carefully hand-ing them one at a time to her assistant in the wings, Busty climbed up on the bed and lay down on her back. Her long shapely legs stuck high in the air and formed a V. This sure was an interesting twist. Our mouths dropped open as we looked at each other in amazement. She wiggled and writhed and thrashed her legs as if in the depths of passion. It was almost like she was having sex with an invisible man. Wow!

I couldn't help notice and marvel at the fact that even though Busty was lying flat on her back, her breasts were standing up tall and pointing toward the ceiling. I wondered how they could possibly do that in apparent defiance of the pull of gravity. I figured out later that Busty must have had what they called breast implants, something still uncommon back in those days. As she brought her faked ecstasy to a climax, I almost expected to hear the sirens as the police pulled up outside the Fox. If her act didn't trigger a raid, I didn't know what would.

Despite Busty being such a tough act to follow, another stripper came out and started into her number. I had a strong suspicion that it was the first girl we had seen strip who was back again in a wig and another outfit. After she took her dress off, I noticed she had a bruise on her thigh the exact same size and in the exact same position as the one I'd noticed on Dixie's leg earlier in the show. But no one else seemed to notice or to care.

Next, there was a second round of what passed for comedy with the never-popular Sammy and Scurvy. After the cold reception they'd received the first time, it took real guts to come back and face the same audience again. After making it through another series of nasty one-liners and stale wisecracks, the comic duo left the stage after bowing like they'd received a standing ovation. About the only people who even applauded them were Dick and me and one or two others (probably fellow novices).

Then, the band gave its biggest fanfare of the evening and the announcer proudly introduced the star attraction of the evening. She was none other than the world-famous Evelyn West and her "$100,000 Treasure Chest" (and he sure wasn't referring to anything related to pirates). He told the audience that her boobs were so precious they were insured by Lloyd's of London. I don't know if that was a fact, but they were sure the biggest ones I'd ever seen (at least up to that point in my young life). And you could tell they were 100% *real* because they bounced as she strutted back and forth across the stage. I liked them much better than Busty's augmented stiffies.

Evelyn was really top-heavy and her dark brunette, teased-up hair only added to the effect. But she was a real class act. No gum chewing and she looked like she was actually enjoying what she was doing. I guess that's what set her apart as a true headliner. When she started her gyrations the light man in the balcony left the white spot on a little longer than usual and we got a thorough eyeful of all her womanly charms. She looked pretty darn good, but was probably old enough to be my mother, and maybe even older. It was hard to tell her age for sure since she was wearing so much stage makeup.

While I was goggling at her physical assets, Dick nudged me and whispered, "Look at that guy up in the box seat." I pulled my eyeballs off Evelyn long enough to quickly glance up at Mr. Raincoat. I couldn't believe what I saw. He had removed his coat and laid it across his lap. His hand was under it and the coat was jumping up and down in a rapid rhythmic manner. Dick and I both knew what he was doing and laughed more than we had at the comedians. The guy must have been in a trance, or so focused on his task that he didn't even notice our laughter. But Evelyn must have and I'm sure she didn't appreciate our distracting guffaws. Even though it was funny, in the back of my mind I was thinking how pathetic this guy was to do such a thing in public. Anyone in the audience could look right up and see him.

Evelyn completed her tantalizing number to the unforgettable tune of "Temptation" with the drummer emphasizing her every energetic bump and slow pelvic grind with heavy beats on the tom-tom. At the very end, she went all the way. Just as the spotlight totally darkened, she yanked off her jewel-encrusted G-string. Wow! Now we had truly seen it ALL—but only for about as long as it takes to blink your eyes. And to keep things legal, she probably had another even smaller crotch covering on under the one she removed. We would never know. Our fertile imaginations supplied the missing details that our eyes hadn't actually been able to see.

As the curtains closed, the house lights came back on, and the pit band knocked out one last song as the audience members trudged up the aisles toward the exits. We sat there a minute or two so as not to have to mingle with the crowd. When we stood up to leave, the musicians finished and began exiting the pit. I'd swear the pianist and the horn player were Sammy and Scurvy. I mentioned it to Dick, but he didn't get a good look at them before they ducked out the pit door. I figured they must perform multiple jobs to help keep expenses down so the Fox could remain in business.

We hurried through the lobby and I pushed the door open with my elbow so I wouldn't touch the same handle that Mr. Raincoat might have touched on his way out. It was raining lightly as we hustled around the corner and back to Dick's car. As I inhaled the misty air it smelled fresh and clean. I'd been glad when we came to the Fox, but now I was even happier to get out of the place. And so ended our big foray into the wicked world of theater burlesque before it passed forever into oblivion.

The strippers we saw at the Fox weren't bad looking (for their age), but their acts were probably pretty tame when compared with the erotic routines of the topless and bottomless pole-dancers and lap-dancers in today's so-called "gentlemen's clubs" (not that I've ever been in one to know). But, to Dick and me, those foxy vixens we saw that night were the epitome of hot, raw flesh and they gave us a thrill like none we'd ever had before. We relived our experience for several days afterward by rehashing all the details and sharing them with our less-adventuresome buddies. Yeah, we'd earned bragging rights and were real heroes to the rest of the guys because we'd been to the Fox. Later, we kicked around the idea of going again. But, after thinking it over, we both agreed that once was enough . . . *more* than enough.

Regular live burlesque shows ended a few years later, but the Fox Theater stayed in business by showing adult films with occasional special live performances. The doors closed forever in 1975 marking the end of an era in Indianapolis and the death of an art form in entertainment history. The building housing the Fox was eventually demolished to clear the block for construction of the American United Life office building.

29

Adventures on the I.T.S.

Most large cities today are served by mass transit systems that move large numbers of people from outlying areas into and out of the city center. These include subways, monorails, commuter trains (some elevated, some ultra-high speed), and high-capacity, surface-level vehicles. But back in the late 1800s, the first mass transit system serving the city of Indianapolis—the Citizens Street Railway Company—used *mule-drawn* streetcars running on tracks to transport riders. This era was way, way before my time. I only mention it for historical interest.

The same streetcar tracks in Indianapolis were later used and expanded to other parts of the growing city by the English Trolley Coach Company. It replaced the old mule-powered streetcars with more "modern" ones that were electric-powered. In my earliest recollections of going uptown with my parents as a very young child, I can remember seeing streetcars running along on steel rails like train tracks down the center of certain streets. Each streetcar had a long, swiveling pickup rod spring-mounted on the roof. This pickup ran along an overhead electrical cable suspended above the tracks to provide power to the streetcar's direct current motor.

Eventually, the electric streetcars were retired and replaced with trackless trolley cars. These looked like modern buses and ran on rubber tires, but still utilized overhead trolleys and cables to power their alternating current electric motors. These vehicles were ahead of their time because they were environmentally friendly—they were quiet and emitted no exhaust fumes. They would've been ideal for use in today's pollution-conscious world. Some of the old steel streetcar tracks were still visible along certain brick streets for several years after they were no longer needed. Eventually, they were all removed or paved over.

The first time I ever rode on a trolley car was when Mary Ellen Craig and I went uptown together. Mary Ellen was a neighbor who lived just two doors north of us on Wright Street. We'd both been chosen by our teachers to participate in a series of art enrichment classes for promising students. The classes were held on certain Saturdays at the John Herron Art Museum. I'd never been uptown unless with my parents, so was sure glad I could go with Mary Ellen. Getting to the museum was a little scary because it required transferring buses on, of all places, Monument Circle—the busy hub of the entire city. Even though we were both in the freshman class at Manual, I'll have to admit that Mary Ellen was more mature for her age than I was. I almost felt like she was my guardian angel. We soon became friends during our Saturday trips together on the trolleys. She made them a fun time of adventure. Once, when she couldn't make it to class and I had to go alone, I sure missed her company.

After I quit riding my bicycle to Manual during my second semester as a freshman, I began riding the trolley cars that ran the route up and down South East Street. As a high school student, I got a pass at school that allowed me to ride on school days for only a dime each way. That was pretty cheap transportation even back then. The very first time I rode the trolley to Manual, I got on and didn't have a dime with me. So, what did I do? Without thinking, I dropped a folded-up dollar bill into the fare box. Uh-oh! The driver immediately let me know that I'd done the *wrong* thing and that I was *supposed* to get change from him and only deposit the *exact fare* into the box. I was so embarrassed. All the people on the trolley—and especially the other kids waiting behind me to pay their fares—were listening to his chastising words and had to be thinking what a dummy I was. I hadn't noticed the little reminder sign on the coin box that said EXACT FARE ONLY. I never made that mistake again, believe me.

Occasionally, the long double-arm trolley apparatus on the roof would jump off the wires and the trolley car would coast to a stop. The driver would turn around and say, "Sorry, folks. I'll be right back." He'd go out the front door and hurry to the rear of the car. Then, he'd reach up with both hands and grab two parallel ropes that hung down from the overhead arms, swing them over, and position them back on the twin overhead cables. When he did, sparks would fly off the wires as he reconnected to the electrical circuit. As soon as he re-entered the trolley and took his seat, off we'd go again. I never figured out what made the trolleys jump off the cables. At least it was only a minor inconvenience, didn't happen often, and was quickly and easily corrected.

The trolley cars were taken out of service in 1955. They were replaced with diesel-engine buses operated by the I.T.S., the Indianapolis Transit System. All the overhead cables and steel supporting poles were eventually taken down. Their removal sure must have created a lot of scrap metal. It also gave the streets a much more open look.

Luckily for me, Wright Street was about halfway between South East Street and Shelby Street. Both were busy thoroughfares and had bus routes running along them. This gave me a choice of two buses to ride and was real handy at times. When headed uptown, I usually walked over to East Street and caught the bus there because it was a block or so closer than Shelby. But, if I was uptown, missed the East Street bus, and was in a hurry, I could catch the one going down Shelby in just a few minutes. Riding the bus required a lot of walking to and from the bus stops, but that was okay. I may have had wienie arms, but I'd developed strong legs during my years of bike riding, so didn't mind the exercise. It was good for me.

When I started dating Joyce Van Lue, who became my high school sweetheart, it was almost entirely via the I.T.S. I figured she must *really* love me because she was willing to ride the bus on our dates. This wasn't such a social stigma back then, but it obviously wasn't a young couple's first choice for transportation. I depended mostly on the I.T.S. for my transportation, along with rides from my dad and Joyce's father once in a while, plus an occasional double date with buddies who owned cars.

Riding the bus on dates did have certain advantages to a boy madly in love. Since I wasn't driving, I could devote full attention to my sweetie. I could sit with my arm around her, hold her hand, look into her eyes, and kiss her while the bus driver took care of getting us where we were going. On some Saturdays, I'd meet Joyce uptown when she got off work at Woolworth's on Washington Street. We'd walk around the corner and down Meridian Street for half a block to Russet's Cafeteria. Or, sometimes, we'd cross Washington Street to Craig's on the corner and have a burger and fries, followed by one of their yummy Persian nut sundaes (boy, were they good). After enjoying a meal together, we'd walk to one of the several downtown theaters and see a movie. Afterward, we'd walk to the bus stop in front of the Banner-Whitehill Furniture Store on South Meridian and wait for the bus. If we had a few extra minutes, we'd spend them looking at the window displays and pointing out what furniture we liked and didn't like. After we casually worked our way as far back as we could go in the recessed entry of the store (which was closed for the day by then), we'd do a little hugging and kissing where people out on the sidewalk wouldn't notice us. Public displays of affection was frowned upon in those days if they went beyond the hand-holding or arm-around stage.

We always rode the Beech Grove bus to Joyce's house. This route went down South East Street, then turned and headed east on Raymond Street. We got off at St. Peter Street, a block west of Keystone Avenue. From there it was only a block and a half walk down to her house. On most Saturday nights, I'd stay as late as I possibly could and catch the very last bus leaving Beech Grove and coming back across Raymond as it headed uptown. At least that's what happened *most* of the time, with a few notable exceptions.

One Saturday night I was a few minutes late leaving Joyce's house and ran like crazy up to Raymond Street. Imagine my relief when I found the bus sitting there at the bus stop. As it turned out, the bus driver was waiting for me. That late at night few people rode the bus and he said he didn't remember me riding home earlier, so figured I must be catching the last bus. What a nice guy he was to be so considerate. Maybe he'd depended on public transportation when he was a young man dating and knew what it was like.

I was his only passenger, so we got to talking and introduced ourselves to one another. His name was Otis. From then on, whenever I rode on the bus and he was driving, I felt like I was riding with a friend. On our next date night, I introduced Joyce to Otis and after that whenever we boarded his bus, he'd greet us with a friendly, "Hi, kids. How are you tonight?" After I dropped our fares in the coin box, he'd say to me, "Now don't you two lovebirds do too much kissin' back there," and give me a big wink. Otis could see us in his oversize rearview mirror, so he knew what we were up to. But he never said anything to interrupt us in our romantic moments.

On another Saturday night when Otis *wasn't* driving the route, I left Joyce's a little too late and missed the bus. I saw it whiz by on

Raymond when I was still half a block away. Darn! Then, I knew I had a long walk of over two miles ahead of me. I'd only gone a couple of blocks across Raymond and was approaching a dark side street when a car pulled up and stopped while I crossed. The driver rolled the window down and shouted, "Hey, Chuck, is that you?" The voice sounded slightly familiar. I walked over to the car and discovered it was John Thicksten, a fellow senior from Manual.

Relieved, I said, "Hi, John. Yeah, it's me." He'd just left his girlfriend's house and was on his way home.

"Where you headed, so late?" he asked.

"Oh, I just missed the last bus and I'm walking home."

"Jump in. I'll give you a ride."

"It's kind of out of your way; I live up near Fountain Square."

John said it wasn't that far and drove me clear to my house. I offered him a buck for gas, but he wouldn't even take it. What a pal. You might think I would've learned my lesson by then, but the powerful attraction of spending every possible minute with a beautiful girl in my arms who couldn't get enough of my kisses was hard to pull myself away from. Can anyone blame me? So, on still another Saturday night, I was again pushing the time for the last bus to come. I hurried to the bus stop and waited . . . and waited . . . and waited. It was really beginning to look like I'd missed the last bus for sure. While I was standing there wondering whether to wait or start walking, a lone car pulled over to the curb. No, it wasn't John Thicksten—or anyone else I knew. *It was a total stranger*. He leaned over, cranked down the window, and asked me if I needed a ride. I knew it wasn't a good idea to accept a ride from someone I didn't know, especially late at night on a nearly deserted street. But I was getting desperate and it was really cold that night. I hesitated, then answered, "Yeah, I think I missed the last bus."

The man said, "Where do you need to go?"

I didn't want to tell him exactly, so just said, "Up near Fountain Square."

He replied, "Well, I'm heading up Shelby Street, so that's no trouble." I was thinking what a fortunate coincidence that he was going my way. But then a little voice in my mind told me that maybe he was just saying that to get me in his car. I hesitated while my mind was bouncing back and forth between the two alternatives: Would it be a short, warm ride or a long, cold walk home? A gust of frigid wind now blowing snowflakes helped me decide. I opted to take a chance and accept a ride. I thanked the man as I climbed in the front seat and rolled up the window. He looked like a normal, decent guy. But you never knew who might be a weirdo.

People in general were more trustworthy in those days, so I thought my odds of getting home safely were fairly good. I decided, however, that if he *didn't* turn and go up Shelby Street, I'd jump out at the first stoplight and run like crazy. I kept my hand near the door handle as we approached Shelby. To my great relief, the man turned right and headed north on Shelby toward Fountain Square. I figured he was okay and relaxed a little.

As we went up Shelby, the snow started coming down heavier and was sticking. The man said he'd take me to my house, but I told him thanks anyway and that he could just let me out at Sanders Street and I'd walk the rest of the way home. He pulled over to the curb at the Teamster's Union Building that sat on the corner. As I got out of the car, I thanked the man again. I inhaled a big gulp of cold air and felt relieved as he pulled away and headed on up the street. Shelby was starting to get slick as I crossed it and began my four-block walk along Sanders. Sure wished I'd worn a hat. The snow was building up on my flattop haircut and I had to keep brushing it off.

I hurried along because it was way after the weekend curfew. In those days, the police could pick up kids who were out on the streets late at night, but they rarely did so unless someone called in and made a complaint. No cruiser came along that night and I finally arrived home, cold but safe. I entered the front door quietly so I wouldn't wake anyone (I also didn't want my folks to see how late I was getting home). I tiptoed up the creaking wooden stairs to my room, changed into my pajamas, and slid under the covers. As I was lying there in the dark before going to sleep, I thought back over the evening's events. I vowed to myself never again to risk riding with a stranger. But, oh, the things we do for love.

After riding the city buses for a year or so longer, Joyce and I became engaged but hadn't set a date for our wedding. I found out later that Joyce's mother had told her, "You're not marrying that boy until he gets a car." I don't remember if Joyce shared this secret ultimatum with me right after receiving it, or some time later after I'd already bought my first set of wheels. In any case, I purchased a 1956 Ford Customline two-door hardtop and our bus-riding days were over. Now, I could stay late on Saturday nights at Joyce's and not have to worry about catching—or missing—the last bus.

Three months later we were married.

My Ford was an unusual green color which by an odd coincidence nearly matched the paint on the furniture in my bedroom (as mentioned in my previous book *Remembering Wright Street*). The car was barely three years old when I bought it off a used car lot for $900 cash. It had the three things that every young man wanted in a car: dual exhausts, whitewall tires, and a push-button radio.

30

A True Love Story

Manual was one of the largest high schools in the city of Indianapolis. As such it had lots and lots of cute girls in attendance. Even though I was never much of a Romeo when it came to dating, I had my share of dates throughout high school. My only problem was that they were all just one-date situations. The girls I dated were all attractive and nice and I certainly could have continued my relationship with them. My fear, however, was that if I dated a girl more than once it would be interpreted as being interested in her and the talk would soon get around school that we had become a couple. For some reason, I just never wanted to settle down with any one girl at the cost of being unable to date any other. That is, not until I met one very special girl during my senior year.

I knew she wasn't a senior, but that didn't matter because to me she was the cutest thing on two legs. I'd pass her in the school hallways occasionally and she always caught my eye. As we passed one another, I never seemed to be in the right position at the right time to speak to her. Several times when I saw her, she was with a certain boy, who I rightly assumed was her boyfriend. So, I took no chances and observed the unwritten "hands-off" rule.

This particular girl and I had no classes together because she was a junior and I was a senior. The only class we might have had in common was typing, but there were lots of typing classes and our schedules never brought us together in any of them. On the first day of my second semester as a senior, my luck changed for the better. I walked into the room assigned for Driver's Education class with Mr. Jack Foster as the instructor . . . and there she sat right in the center of the classroom. There was an empty desk in the row next to hers and I quickly headed for it.

I ended up sitting beside another girl named Willodyne Quarles. She was a junior I knew slightly as an acquaintance of my sister, Sandy. Willy, as most people called her, was also a graduate of good old P. S. #18, my grade school alma mater. She seemed to know the cute girl sitting behind her because I saw them talking when I entered the room. After I sat down, Willy and I chatted for a minute before Mr. Foster came in. I asked Willy who her friend was. She introduced me to Joyce Ann Van Lue. Joyce sort of smiled at me and said, "Hi." I smiled real big at her, and said, "Hi" back. I noticed that she had a mouth full of braces on her teeth, but

I still thought she was the cutest girl I'd ever seen. I wasn't sure why, but it was like she was made just for me. Unfortunately, some other guy didn't know that and he had found her first.

Mr. Foster soon arrived and we got down to our first lesson in the basics of learning how to drive a car. The course involved both classroom instruction and practice driving in a dual-control car. Each person in the class was assigned to a group of three or four students. The groups would meet Mr. Foster or Mr. Moriarty, the other driving teacher, during free periods according to an elaborate schedule. We'd take turns behind the wheel on a rotating basis, so that we all got some actual driving experience (mostly around nearby Garfield Park). In those days you learned how to drive in a car with a stick shift (that means it had a *manual* transmission and you had to shift through the gears every time you took off). But enough about that. My big disappointment was that Joyce, the cute girl, was *not* in my driving group. I had Foster; she had Moriarty. Rats!

One day when I came into the Driver's Ed classroom (and I always tried to get there as quickly as possible), I immediately noticed that Joyce was crying. Since I still hadn't broken the ice with her as far as carrying on a real conversation, I asked my friend Willy what was going on. She whispered to me that Joyce and her boyfriend had just broken up. So that explained her tears. I honestly felt sorry for Joyce, but at the same time I was inwardly glad about the cause of her sadness. I know that makes me sound like a heel, but it's the truth. Now, Joyce was fair game. I flashed a sympathetic look at her across the aisle while she was wiping her eyes and trying to compose herself before class started. It was the first step in making my move.

Every year the Roines had a combination hayride and wiener roast. The Roines (that's "senior" spelled backwards) was an honor club for senior boys who had excellent scholastics and were, in general, a credit to the school. This was a select group; total membership my senior year was only eighteen—and I was proud to be one of them. The group's sponsor for many years had been Miss Garnett Foreman. She was a sweetie, but had to retire due to poor health. Mr. Richard Blough took over as our faculty sponsor. He was a real fun guy and was well-liked by everyone.

I had no idea who I was going to ask to our annual event. It wasn't easy to ask a girl you'd never dated before to go on a hayride. The other Roines guys who had steady girls would all be hugging and holding hands and sneaking an occasional kiss from their dates. I certainly didn't expect a girl I'd never dated before to engage in such romantic expressions. I figured that most girls probably wouldn't even want to go on a hayride on a first date because such things would likely be going on. But, in my mind, the name of the only girl I really wanted to ask rose to the surface above all others: Joyce Van Lue. A few days had gone by and she'd had time to get over her recent breakup. I wanted to move fast before any other boys got similar ideas and tried to make moves on her.

I asked Willy to get Joyce's phone number for me. I figured that if Joyce wouldn't give her number to Willy it would be a definite sign that she had no interest in going out with me. If, on the other hand, she *did* give Willy her phone number it was a mighty good sign that she was interested in a date. The next day in Driver's Ed, Willy slipped me a little folded-up piece of paper. I knew what it was, but when I unfolded it and saw that magic number ST6-6894, my heart skipped a beat.

I called Joyce that night and asked her about going to the hayride and wiener roast. She said she'd like to but had to ask her folks. She left the phone for a couple of minutes while I hung on straining to hear any possible conversation in the background. When Joyce came back on the phone, her answer was, "Yes, I can go." I nearly shouted, "Yippeeee!" but managed to control myself. I told her the details and got her address. I'd already checked with Paul Schnepf, a buddy in Roines, and he said I could double-date with him and his girl, Linda Schultz.

On the following Friday night, Paul and Linda picked me up at my house. I was really excited as we drove over to Joyce's. When we got there, I went inside and met her folks. Her younger sister and little brother hung in the background looking me over. I guess I passed everyone's inspection because they actually allowed me the privilege and pleasure of leaving with Joyce in tow. Right from the first, she was so easy to talk to that I felt like I'd known her for years. I could tell immediately that this was going to be a date to remember.

Joyce and I started getting acquainted on the way and we soon arrived at the Silver Hills Riding Stables out on Southeastern Avenue. After a few minutes, everyone had arrived and we all climbed aboard the horse-drawn hay wagon. The evening was chilly with a light mist in the air. But that didn't dampen anyone's enthusiasm. The wagon driver had brought along enough blankets for one per couple. We put them over us to help stay dry. Since we were sharing a blanket, I had a good excuse to snuggle up close to Joyce. There was a lot of cutting up and joking around along the way. We all sang a few songs, and now and then did a bit of smooching—except Joyce and me. We didn't since it was our first time to go out together (guys and gals back then usually didn't kiss on their first date). I did manage to put my arm around her in a protective way as we bounced along in the old wooden wagon. She didn't seem to mind. I was in heaven.

After making the rounds on the hayride, the rain let up and we returned to a roaring campfire. It helped dry us out as we roasted wieners and marshmallows, and continued the evening of fun. I'd never felt so at ease with a girl in my life. I didn't have to worry about what to say or how to act. I could just be myself. And myself was okay with her.

All too soon the evening came to an end. Paul drove us back to Joyce's house. As I walked her up to the door I was thinking (like every boy does), *Should I kiss her goodnight or not?* The question was answered for me. Joyce kind of lingered outside her front door and I could somehow sense that it would be alright. I leaned over and kissed her lightly on the cheek. As I drew back our eyes met and I knew that wasn't enough for either of us. Our lips met in a tender kiss—and my fate was sealed. I was instantly and forever head over heels in love with Joyce Van Lue. And I guess, as it turned out, the feeling was mutual.

Right after that, we started dating regularly. On our second date, Joyce asked me if I would mind if she called me Chuck. Of course, I had no objections—she could call me whatever she wanted. My family had always called me Charles. My parents would sometimes call me by my full name, Charles Edward, but when they did I knew I was in trouble of some kind. My friends and other acquaintances usually called me Charlie; a few even called me Chaz. Joyce said she thought Charles was too formal and that Charlie and Chaz just didn't fit my personality. So, Chuck it was from then on. I liked it and it has stuck with me through all the years since we met.

Just a few weeks later I asked Joyce to go steady and offered her my senior class ring as a token of my commitment to her. When she accepted it, I think there may have been a tiny tear in the corner of her eye. I know there was a big lump in my throat. The ring was way too large for her, so she followed the prevailing custom of the time and wrapped the narrow part with a bunch of adhesive tape, then painted the tape ball with fingernail polish to match her nails. Wearing a senior boy's ring was every high school girl's dream in the '50s.

Joyce and I saw each other every weekend from then on, often two or three times. During the week, I'd call her each evening and we'd talk for at least half an hour. The rest of my senior year flew by. After graduating from Manual, I went off to Flint, Michigan, to be a student at General Motors Institute. They were going to turn me into a mechanical engineer (at least they tried). Joyce finished her last year of high school and didn't even get to attend her senior prom because I was away in Flint. Now, that's true love for you.

After discovering that I really didn't want to be an engineer, I dropped out of G.M.I., came back to Indianapolis, and returned to my former job with the civil engineering and surveying company I'd worked for while a senior and during the summer. It wasn't long before I took my class ring back and gave Joyce an engagement ring in its place. I'd even sat down with her father in the traditional way before popping the question to her and asked him for her hand in marriage. He said it would be fine and that he and Joyce's mother would be proud to have me as their son-in-law. When I showed Joyce the ring and asked her the big question, she said yes without hesitation. At the moment I slipped the ring on her finger, she was the happiest girl on earth. And I was the happiest boy.

I knew I had a real knockout for a fiancée. But I developed a bit of a jealous streak—okay, it was a *big* jealous streak—that showed itself after we'd been engaged for six months or so. This caused some friction in our relationship, but I kept it under control and we stayed together. I think it may have been sexual tension from wanting her and not being able to have her until we were married. I know that sounds ridiculously old-fashioned in today's times, but it was the way things were back then for most young people. Chastity and abstinence were the general rule. No sex before marriage; no living together to see if we were compatible; no honeymoon before the marriage. In other words: no wedding, no bedding.

Several months later I obtained an even better job with a great future at the Indianapolis Power & Light Company. I eventually bought my first car (just three months before our wedding). A little over a year after becoming engaged, we were married at the Olive Branch Christian Church on the hottest day in the month of August 1959. Sure, it was tough waiting to have sex until after we were married, but it made the waiting all the more worthwhile when it was finally time for our honeymoon. Oh, baby, it was worth the wait.

On August 16, 2009, we celebrated our fiftieth wedding anniversary after a lifetime of marriage, raising four wonderful children, and being blessed with six darling grandkids. And it all started at Manual High School way back in 1957 when a shy boy from Wright Street met a cute girl from St. Peter Street in Driver's Education class. They began their hand-in-hand journey through life then and they continue it today . . . together.

Joyce and I on the night of my Senior Prom. What a cutie! Check out that plaid trim.

My true love and I ready to go do some dancing at the Indiana Roof Ballroom.

APPENDICES

Appendix A

Fun and Games

Childhood is the time when fun and games occupy a major portion of our life. Activities that kids consider enjoyable may change over the decades, but some have remained favorites no matter what the year on the calendar. Following is a random, non-inclusive listing of many of the games we played and other things we did "just for the fun of it" while I was growing up. Some of these were boy-related, some were for girls. Others were enjoyed by both. If parts of the list seem a little "boy heavy" you'll understand why.

INDOOR GAMES

Checkers . . . Chinese checkers . . . Old Maid . . . pickup sticks . . . Cootie . . . Operation . . . charades . . . twenty questions . . . spin the bottle (a kissing game) . . . post office (another kissing game) . . . pin the tail on the donkey (always a birthday party favorite) . . . drop the (wooden) clothespins into the (glass) milk bottle . . . battleship (using graph paper) . . . the gossip game . . . Parcheesi . . . dominoes . . . ping-pong . . . making shadow images of animals, birds, and people on the wall with your hands . . . darts . . . hangman . . . connect the dots . . . battle tops . . . tiddlywinks . . . Slinky . . . talking to each other on a "telephone" made of two tin cans connected with a long piece of tightly stretched string.

OUTDOOR GAMES AND ACTIVITIES

Red rover . . . tag . . . freeze tag . . . hide and seek . . . jacks . . . mumblety-peg (never played, but watched) . . . shooting marbles . . . dodge ball . . . hopscotch . . . cowboys and Indians . . . war . . . water pistols . . . cap guns . . . horse (a two-person basketball shooting competition) . . . flies and grounders . . . roller-skating . . . riding bikes . . . riding scooters . . . riding wagons . . . bouncing on a pogo stick . . . walking on stilts (made either of wood or from tin cans tied onto string loops) . . . burning ants with a magnifying glass . . . spitting watermelon seeds (at each other or at a target) . . . apple core-Baltimore . . . swimming (whether in a pool or in the "old swimming hole") . . . pitching horseshoes . . . badminton . . . croquet . . . Chinese yo-yo . . . spitting contests . . . making and flying kites . . . flying balsawood gliders . . . sledding . . . ice-skating . . . making a snowman . . . building a snow fort . . . snowball fights . . . touch football . . . pickup basketball games (usually with a netless hoop mounted on the garage roof in the alley behind some kid's house) . . . building and racing pushmobiles . . . building a car and entering the Soap Box Derby (I never did this, but knew a kid who did) . . . building and flying model airplanes . . . going on a family picnic . . . hunting for crawdads in Pleasant Run . . . shooting cans, bottles, or rats at a dump with a BB gun or an air rifle . . . setting off fireworks (back when they were legal) . . . building a raft and floating it down a creek or river or on a pond or lake . . . skipping flat stones across the surface of whatever body of water was handy . . . leapfrog . . . walking on your hands (I could never do this) . . . riding a unicycle (never had one, but a kid in our neighborhood did) . . . plinking things with a slingshot you made yourself from a fork cut out of a dead tree limb . . . soaping windows at Halloween (not guilty) . . . lighting a sack of dog poop on someone's front porch, ringing their doorbell, and watching the fun as they run outside and stomp out the fire (a really mean Halloween trick I'm definitely *not* guilty of, only heard about this one) . . . making S'Mores over a campfire . . . hunting for four-leaf clovers . . . making necklaces out of long-stemmed clover flowers . . . gathering a bouquet of dandelions and proudly presenting them to your mother . . . marveling at the discarded outer skins of cicadas that came out of the ground every so many years and made an awful screeching sound for several days . . .

blowing soap bubbles . . . playing catch (with a baseball, a softball, or a football) . . . catching lightning bugs and putting them in a glass jar . . . pitching pennies . . . playing in a sandbox . . . throwing a camp-bomb up in the air and hearing it go off with a bang when it hit the sidewalk or street (or a neighbor's parked car).

OTHER FUN STUFF AND ACTIVITIES

Making and flying paper airplanes . . . blowing plastic bubbles . . . making and shooting rubber band guns . . . playing with Mexican jumping beans . . . pet chameleons (came with a little gold chain to pin them on your shirt or blouse) . . . fake vomit . . . fake dog poop . . . fake sore thumb . . . playing with paper dolls . . . coloring books . . . paddle and ball . . . practical jokes (like snakes in a can, whoopee cushions, and hand buzzers) . . . Hula-Hoops . . . Riddly-diddly-diddly-dee (a guessing game) . . . reading . . . cootie catchers . . . shrunken heads . . . drawing . . . collecting stuff (whether it was rocks, bottle caps, match flaps, cigar bands, or whatever caught our fancy) . . . collecting and trading bubblegum cards (featuring baseball players and other sports figures, World War II airplanes, movie stars, etc.) . . . playing April fool jokes on other kids . . . yelling "pokes" when another kid belched or farted and then punching them in the forearm unless they yelled "vent pokes" first . . . yelling "jinx, you owe me a Coke" when you and another kid said the same thing at the same time . . . going to the Penny Arcade (remember the Test Your Strength machines, fortune teller machines, photograph card machines, and the war-related shoot the Jap or Kraut machines?) . . . going to carnivals . . . going to a big three-ring circus put on in a huge tent . . . going to the zoo (this meant a trip to Cincinnati) . . . going to a local amusement park like Riverside (back before Disney started the trend toward the giant super-parks) . . . making dares to other kids and doing dares made to you . . . yo-yos . . . scavenger hunts . . . playing with dolls . . . playing dress up . . . trick-or-treating at Halloween with costumes made up of odds and ends you found at home . . . building a house out of cards . . . sneaking up behind someone and scaring them by popping a small paper bag you'd blown up with air . . . teaching your dog a new trick . . . playing with your pet monkey (if you were lucky enough to have one—I never did, but always wanted one) . . . having a dog who gave birth to a litter of pups or a cat that had a litter of kittens . . . blindman's buff (or, bluff) . . . peashooters (a.k.a., beanshooters) . . . decorating and wearing a beanie (with or without a propeller on top . . . customizing your bike (maybe by sticking bottle caps in the spokes or adding some accessory you bought at Blue Point) . . . going to birthday parties . . . watching Punch and Judy puppet shows . . . telling scary ghost stories . . . clackers . . . Mother, May I? . . . Simon Says . . . playing a kazoo . . . ring toss . . . rock, paper, scissors with winner slapping the back of the loser's hand . . . flinch . . . ant farms . . . playing with a gyroscope (sort of a modern version of a top, but you could do several different tricks with it) . . . going to summer camp . . . short sheeting someone's bed at camp . . . putting acorns or pine cones in someone's bunk at camp . . . dipping someone's hand in warm water while they're asleep and making them pee in their bed . . . various athletic programs at Southside Turners . . . Cub Scouts . . . Webelos . . . Boy Scouts . . . Brownies . . . Girl Scouts . . . Bluebirds . . . Campfire Girls . . . P.A.L. Club . . . Golden Gloves (a boxing organization for boys) . . . Boy's Club of America . . . Girl's Club of America.

Did we have lots of fun? Boy, did we ever.

Appendix B

Grade School Memories

Here are some miscellaneous memories from my days at Abraham Lincoln School #18 (I went there from the sixth through the eighth grades). If you, too, went to P. S. #18, see how many of these you remember. Even if you went to another elementary school, you may have similar memories.

Standing in rows with hands over hearts and reciting the Pledge of Allegiance every morning before classes started . . . walking around Pleasant Run Parkway from the school to a certain grove of trees in Garfield Park on the south side of Raymond Street, just west of South East Street, to participate in National Arbor Day programs (this was considered a big field trip in those days) . . . listening to "morning music" as famous classical selections were played on a big old, hand-cranked Victrola in the second-floor hallway while the students sat quietly in their classrooms with the doors open so they could hear (no P.A. system back then) . . . participating in or just watching the special foot races and other athletic events that were part of the annual May Day observances . . . going down to the basement and all the girls heading into the Home Economics room (with its screen door to keep the flies out) and the boys all heading into the big shop area . . . laboriously re-casing tiny pieces of lead type that were used in various projects in the Print Shop (or just dumping them inside the cabinet) . . . bent over using a beat-up old drawing board laid flat on top of a workbench during Mechanical Drawing class (the boards were full of thumbtack holes from being in use for decades) . . . the smell of melting solder in Metal Shop . . . designing and making various projects in Wood Shop, then taking them home and proudly showing them to your parents . . . participating in the annual spelling bees . . . going to the auditorium on Fridays and the entire school singing songs and choruses together . . . stopping at Newman's Market (right across the street from the school) to buy candy . . . walking to and from school *twice* daily on school days (no lunch was served at school) . . . going to the basement for morning milk and enjoying your glass bottle of white milk along with one Graham cracker and one soda cracker (what a treat) . . . hearing the noise of the empty glass bottles being returned to the heavy wood-and-metal carrying racks . . . preparing science notebooks every six weeks for Miss Norma Cook's science class (they had to have ten pictures and ten write-ups) . . . passing Mr. Jackson, the school principal, in the halls with a certain amount of awe (he was at least six feet tall and always had a ruddy complexion) . . . hearing rumors about such-and-such a kid having to go to the principal's office and getting a paddling for some misdeed (yes, they still used the paddle in those days, or so I heard) . . . marveling at the *green* chalkboards and yellow chalk used in the new addition to the school (we thought they only came in *black* with *white* chalk) . . . being assigned to take the dusty chalkboard erasers out back of the school building and clopping them together to beat the chalk dust out of them (had to be careful which way the wind was blowing or you'd end up with it all over you) . . . being assigned to fill the ink wells at each desk from a big glass bottle with a special spout on the end . . . seeing an ink well bubble over because some prankster dropped an Alka-Seltzer tablet into it when no one was looking (no, it wasn't me) . . . jumping under your desk and covering your head and neck with your arms in "duck and cover" drills required as part of Civil Defense (to help protect us from atomic bombs that the dreaded Russians might drop on us) . . . participating in the chalkboard mathematics competitions Mrs. Lucy Swisher would conduct between the boys and the girls (was it my imagination or did she look exactly like the ill-tempered Queen of Hearts in the old original illustrations for *Alice in Wonderland*?) . . . looking at all the glass jars full of weird things in the cabinets in Miss Koch's science classroom . . . playing out on the gravel-covered playground behind the school . . . watching some of the better hitters during gym class softball games try to put one through Mr. Jackson's office window . . . attending health classes in the new classroom on the northwest corner of the building addition . . . seeing the girls in their blue gymsuits as they ran across the hall from their changing room to the gym . . . singing "Good King Wenceslaus" and other traditional favorites in the annual school Christmas program . . . having music classes conducted by the young and pretty Miss Mary Trapp (who was actually related to the famous singing Von Trapp family of *The Sound of Music* fame) . . . being forbidden to ever go up the second-floor stairway to the old gym located on the third floor under the roof (it was closed after the new gym was built) . . . being told about how a tribe of Delaware Indians once lived on the site where the school was built (a bronze plaque beside the main entrance documented the fact) . . . seeing the old white brick house across Palmer Street from the front of the school and wondering why it sat at such an odd angle when all the other houses were aligned squarely with the street (this was supposedly the first brick house built in what became Marion County and there was no street at the time to line it up with) . . . hearing the floors creak as you went up and down the wooden stairs or walked along the wide hallways . . . smelling the freshly polished wood floors on the first day after summer vacation . . . watching your teacher open or close the huge windows in your classroom with a long pole made for this purpose . . . laughing when one of the roller window shades would suddenly for no reason roll up on its own and scare everyone in the class . . . reading all the initials other kids had carved into your desk top over the decades . . . wearing your *black* basketball shoes to gym and wishing you could have *white* ones like some of the other guys . . . evacuating the school during fire drills . . . entering your answers in "truth books" passed around on the sneak and reading what the other kids had said.

"School days, school day, good old Golden Rule days . . ."

Public School #18 as it looked before the 1950 addition onto west end of building (looking toward northwest corner).

Appendix C

High School Memories

Here's a collection of some random memories from my four years at the new Manual High School that were not mentioned elsewhere in this book. A few of these I only heard about and never personally experienced. See how many you remember. Some may be similar to memories of yours no matter where you went to high school.

Standing in lunch line . . . hearing someone's empty lunch tray clatter loudly to the floor after being knocked out of their hand by a prankster and everyone nearby yelling "Freshie !". . . blowing soda straw wrappers dipped in gravy upward so they stuck on the ceiling tiles of the cafeteria like paper stalactites . . . hustling over to the Delavan Smith Athletic Field on Madison Avenue to have outdoor gym class (when weather permitted) . . . running laps around the cinder track at D.S.A.F. . . . going to Friday night football games at D.S.A.F. . . . looking over the top of the wall and watching the marching band come up Pennsylvania Street to the lively cadence of half a dozen snare drummers . . . seeing your friends in the bleachers . . . seeing the hallways plastered with posters for the Student Affairs Board elections . . . going to auditorium programs and getting out of classes early all day on a special schedule . . . watching out the window at people prowling around the edge of the campus along Pleasant Run Parkway while they looked for a hidden treasure in follow-up to a misinterpreted clue given as part of a radio station's ongoing treasure hunt game . . . using those clever pull-out, lockable drawing boards in Mechanical Drawing class . . . hurrying across campus in cold or wet weather to get to and from the gymnasium building . . . seeing the ROTC boys practicing marching and standing formation out in the parking lot . . . stomping on the pull-out wooden bleachers in the gym to show our enthusiasm during pep rallies and at basketball games . . . hearing the Pep Band blast out "Onward, Manual!" during the basketball games . . . seeing the Civil Defense "cops" who acted as chaperoning authority figures at the various dances held in the school cafeteria . . . marveling at the huge circular mosaic design in the floor of the main entry lobby showing all the main areas of study at the school . . . eagerly looking through the Friday issues of *The Booster* school newspaper to catch the latest news . . . having your friends and favorite teachers sign your *Ivian* yearbook so you'd never forget them . . . seeing all the girls wearing skirts to school every day (I'm not even sure we had a school dress code back then, kids just wanted to look their best) . . . standing in line for school pictures and hoping you didn't come out looking too weird . . . seeing the huge voting machines on wheels stored near the entries to the gym in readiness for a coming political election . . . sneaking up to Morgan's Restaurant for an off-campus lunch . . . enjoying the delicious goodies from Carlos Bakery . . . riding your bicycle to school and dragging it down over the huge rocks under the railroad overpass across Pleasant Run creek in Garfield Park . . . stopping at the Sunoco Station on the corner of South East Street and Raymond to buy a candy bar or bottle of pop . . . walking along South East Street and smelling the delicious aroma of catsup and pork and beans in the air from the Stokely Van-Camp canning factory . . . hearing the sound of tin cans rattling across the overhead conveyor running from the American Can Company plant and crossing South East Street to Stokely's . . . watching our marching band's lovely drum majorette, Lois Strong, in her white boots and short, short skirt showing lots of leg while leading the marching band . . . dressing up fancy for Senior Day . . . homecoming football games and all the added hoopla associated with them . . . looking around in the school bookstore to check out the latest items available . . . bringing a written excuse from your parents to the school office before you could be readmitted to classes after an absence . . . showing your student identification card to the bus driver when you got on so you could ride a city bus down South East Street clear to Raymond for only a dime . . . stopping at Pantzer's Pharmacy on the way home to enjoy a cherry coke at their soda fountain . . . taking the shortcut along the footpath running beside Pleasant Run . . . carrying your report card from class to class and anxiously waiting to see what grades your teachers would give you . . . making the Honor Roll . . . earning those little pale blue ribbons for excellence in various subjects . . . watching the Fire Department use their ladder truck to hang the giant Christmas wreath over the main entrance . . . voting for your favorite candidates for homecoming King and Queen . . . following the "pink and black" fashion fad . . . boys' shirts with standup mandarin collars . . . pegged trousers with tight cuffs . . . knit ties . . . flannel suits . . . key chains . . . cuff links . . . I.D. bracelets . . . poodle skirts . . . sleeveless blouses . . . angora collars . . . letting your girlfriend wear your letterman's jacket (or being a girl and getting to wear one) . . . giving your steady girl your class ring to wear (or being a girl and wearing one) . . . going to ballgames at home or away, whether during the regular seasons or during city tournaments or the sectionals, when we played such teams as the Ben Davis "Giants," the Broad Ripple "Rockets," the Cathedral "Irish," the Crispus Attucks "Tigers," the Howe "Hornets," the North Central "Panthers," the Sacred Heart "Spartans," the Scecina "Crusaders," the Shortridge "Blue Devils," the Southport "Cardinals," the Speedway "Sparkplugs," our arch-rivals the Tech "Greenclad," the Warren Central "Warriors," the Washington "Continentals," and the Harry E. Wood "Woodchucks." The Manual "Redskins" played them all and beat most of them most of the time.

"Those were the days my friend, we thought they'd never end . . . "

My senior yearbook photo. Note the flattop haircut that was popular in those days.

Manual High School - Class of 1957
Senior Day class armband logo.

Manual High School – Class of 1957
Senior Day Roines lapel badge logo.

Made in the USA
Charleston, SC
01 May 2011